A WALK AROUND THE BLOCK

LITERARY TEXTS AND SOCIAL CONTEXTS

Eugene Paul Nassar

Ethnic Heritage Studies Center
Utica College of Syracuse University
1999

Copyright © 1999 by Eugene Paul Nassar

Going away can be like falling in the ocean.
Or like a walk around the block, when you've never been away because nothing you've done away has any meaning without your sense of home.
Wind of the Land

also by Eugene Paul Nassar

Wallace Stevens: An Anatomy of Figuration

The *Rape of Cinderella: Essays in Literary Continuity*

The Cantos of Ezra Pound: the Lyric Mode

Wind of the Land (a memoir)

Essays: Critical and Metacritical

Illustrations to Dante's Inferno

To Villagers, Neighborhood and Family People, and Regionalists, everywhere, and, especially to my brother Mike, who shared it all with me.

Contents

1. Symbols and Texts: A Personal Sketch of Literary Criticism Since the Fifties   13

2. The Radiant Core: Family, Village, Neighborhood, and Region in Literature   41

3. Family and Village in Folk Literature: Some Lebanese and Sicilian Examples   113

4. Social Contexts as Poetic Texts   167

Preface

The following essays clearly belong to the end of one's career rather than the beginning. The prose in its ellipticalness and casualness can either be seen as earned, or as late softheadedness. I appeal for the former.

The first essay, which has appeared in the *Virginia Quarterly Review* (67:1), and has incorporated a few paragraphs from reviews of mine in *Essays in Criticism* (38:4), *The Sewanee Review* (95:2), and *Modern Age* (30:2), is a summing up of one who has tried to practice close literary criticism in the style of his former teachers and critical models. In its shamelessly personal focus, it may prepare the reader for the autobiographical quality of the social meditations that follow on familialism and localism in some texts of world and folk literature. These essays argue respect for the unique social context as one ought to respect the unique poetic text. Portions of these latter essays have appeared in *The Syracuse Scholar* (9:2), and *New York Folklore* (10:1). I thank all of the journals mentioned for kind permission to use this material in a revised form and in a new context.

I am grateful to Karen Orr for her skill and patience in entering the manuscript into the computer and retrieving it into page designs, and to Bob Cimbalo for the wonderfully evocative paintings and sketches.

Chapter One

Symbols and Texts: A Personal Sketch of
Literary Criticism Since the Fifties

I take as my text for this essay the delicate and powerful Lebanese folk song my mother often sang in Arabic:

The roses are full, full
The roses are always on my mind.
I love the roses only
And, O my soul, the lettuce leaf.

The peasant (and there is, perhaps, a peasant in all of us) has juxtaposed the roses and the lettuce, both deeply important to his psyche. The singer is withdrawn, and often withdraws, from his daily tribulations into a reverie of the beauty of flowers and the vegetable garden. I remember my mother hanging clothes on the clothesline in our garden at the back of our house, singing as she looked out over the vegetables and fruit trees my father so lovingly cultivated. I have no doubt the song meant a great deal to my mother in part because of her belief that there was a sacred connection between the abundant earth and the God who loved, planned, protected and nurtured, an accessible, understandable Father. The words I use in my memoir, *Wind of the Land*, to convey this symbolic idea are "veins of lettuce leaf flowing into the heart of the Lord".

Whether in my prose or in the poetry of the folk-poet, the symbol of the lettuce leaf takes on its symbolic meaning, power, and value in the unique contexts of language and culture from which it comes. The meanings and the values however are all accessible from the contexts to the willing student from whatever culture. To attempt to interpret either text from the opposite direction, that is, to impose categorical interpretations of the symbols drawn from ideological paradigms, from archetypal roses or lettuce, is to shred the contexts into a most indigestible salad.

William Wimsatt has been, from the beginning of my own serious study of literature, my favorite theoretician (as his partner and peer, Cleanth Brooks, my favorite critic), and no one has been more acute in the making of precise distinctions (much like his own mentor, Samuel Johnson) between abstractions that work and abstractions that do not:

> ...this... shows the abstractionism involved in any attempt to give fixed interpretations to either natural or artificial classes of symbols or to prescribe symbols for given defined meanings. The poet abstracts too in his own way, in his choices and juxtapositions, but he claims for his abstraction only the correctness of his momentary context.
> "Two Meanings of Symbolism"
> *Hateful Contraries* (1965), p.66.

"Momentary context": created by the unique choices and juxtapositions of language and action that constitute the aesthetic text and which generate the moments of unique aesthetic pleasure. The aesthetic moments are accessible only through the accurate understanding of the given context. And if one believes that aesthetic pleasure is a deep and important part of one's life, then the close study of individual texts becomes a discipline worth giving one's meditative life to. To quote Wimsatt again: "The verbal object and its analysis constitute the domain of literary criticism" (*The Verbal Icon*, 1954, p. 232).

The precise understanding of "symbol," and "context," and "literary criticism" that one finds in Wimsatt has often been ignored (to one's own peril) in the deluge of "literary theory" since the mid-fifties and I would like to argue in this chapter and from the perspectives of this volume both the value of and a return to the approaches to literary criticism of both Wimsatt and Brooks.

My Father always called the wind "khai" or "brother" in Arabic, but so did he call "brother" as well ripe grapes or any one of his three sons, testifying to the right relation between brothers in the Lebanese culture of family. That St. Francis speaks in his "Cantico" of "Frate Vento" and "Sora Acqua" testifies to the strain of universal peasant in both my Father and St. Francis, the radiant core of familialism in both. But we are speaking of somewhat universal sentiments, not a universal language or symbology. The symbols of wind, water, or lettuce leaf are present in most peasant or village tale, but their precise valuations in any specific social (and ultimately linguistic) context are as variable as wind and water themselves and need both precise articulation on the part of the author and accurate response on the part of the reader.

What Erich Fromm does to the *Jonah* story and its symbols is *not* literary criticism:

> We find a sequence of symbols which follow one another: going into the ship, going into the ship's belly, falling asleep, being in the ocean, and being in the fish's belly. All these symbols stand for the same inner experience: for a condition of being protected and isolated, of safe withdrawal from communication with other human beings. They represent what could be represented in another symbol, the fetus in the mother's womb. Different as the ship's belly, deep sleep, the ocean, and a fish's belly are realistically, they are expressive of the same inner experience...("The Nature of Symbolic Language," *The Forgotten Language*, 1951).

No matter that in the story (the "manifest" story) Jonah was first escaping from God, then, when confronted by the sailors, repents and is willing to be cast on the waters, then considers his being swallowed by a whale a miraculous rescue by a merciful God--

that is, three very different experiences on Jonah's part--Fromm would have us see all three episodes, in the ship, on the water, and in the belly of the fish as "return to the womb" symbols, symbols ultimately of the writer's neurosis (the true "latent" content), his wish to withdraw. Thus a unique plot is replaced by a repeated platitude, a vivid story by a vague symbology, the author's apparent meaning by the psychoanalyst's paradigm.

Fromm's methodology can stand as representative of a wide spectrum of what is called literary criticism or theory over the past thirty-five years, which is in fact typified by a relative lack of interest in the specific pleasures of the specific text coupled with a fascination for the paradigms one can impose upon a number of texts considered as a set. The paradigm can be from literary theory, from scientific, linguistic or philosophic presumptions, or from political or social ideology. Whatever, the specific poem or story is not treated with the respect one ought to accord to another's home or garden or village, but as an open field for anyone to pick over, strip, scratch, or mine.

I left my family and home and its garden in Upstate New York in 1953 for Kenyon College in the middle of Ohio. I knew nothing then about the fame of the college, only that I was told by a high school teacher that it was a good school in Chemistry and Pre-Medical studies, in which I planned to major, and that this school with Episcopalian connections was willing to give a

Lebanese immigrant mill-worker's son a free tuition scholarship. I stayed with Chemistry and Pre-Medical studies at Kenyon for four years, and finally dropped out of Yale Medical School after a tenure of nine days. But from the first day at Kenyon when the Freshmen were addressed by the President responsible for assembling the college's world-class faculty, Gordon Keith Chalmers, I realized that I was in a magnificent humanistic and scholarly environment of a sort that I had dreamed about as I had read (encouraged by my brother and a few fine teachers) Tolstoy, Dostoyevski, and Shakespeare back in the ethnic neighborhood. Denham Sutcliffe, Charles Coffin, and John Crowe Ransom fired my enthusiasm for Literature, Phillip Blair Rice, Virgil Aldrich, and Wilfred Desan for Philosophy, Richard Salomon and Denis Baly for History, Robert O. Fink for the Classics, Bruce Haywood for German Literature, Bayes Norton for Chemistry, and Otton Martin Nikodym for Mathematics. Ransom's *Kenyon Review* was of course the intellectual focus of the campus, as it was, in large measure, of the literary world of the Forties and Fifties. Because of the *Review*, the campus was always abuzz concerning the current visitor there, Lionel Trilling, Randall Jarrell, Robert Frost, Robert Lowell, etc. to pay homage to Ransom, and perhaps to give a courtesy lecture. And yet I can see Ransom, diminutive and gentlemanly, putting together the *Review* at his desk in a little cubbyhole of an office, with the help of one part-time secretary, and then treating me, as he did all of his students, in class and afterwards, as if my poor writings were the most important thing in his day or week.

I was spending so much time in science laboratories, had so little time for the humanistic studies that I loved or for the conversation that I craved with the humanities majors, that I soon cultivated a survivalist's sense for the essential as opposed to the peripheral, the enduring as opposed to the fashionable, the concrete reality of a text as opposed to the abstract and ideological theorizing about texts.

Ransom's poetry delighted me as did the stimulating pages of the *Review*. Privately, Ransom told me that, if I ever changed my mind about Medicine, Yale was the graduate school for the study of literature for me, and Prof. Cleanth Brooks the man to study with. And change my mind I did. But before I could apply to Yale, Ransom, Sutcliffe, and Nikodym put forward my name for the Rhodes Scholarship, which then brought me instead to Worcester College at Oxford University. There, by another incredible stroke of luck, I was given to a young tutor, Christopher Ricks, who now hardly has a peer in English Studies. Prof. Ricks expressed his pleasure at having a graduate of Kenyon and especially a student of Ransom's as a pupil, and also announced that he was a great admirer of Prof. Wimsatt's *The Verbal Icon* which was among the great number of books of literary criticism and theory that I knew I ought to have, but had not yet read.

Our first tutorial was to be in Shakespeare, and remembering Ransom's recommendation, I sought out a copy of Cleanth Brooks's *Well Wrought Urn* to read the opening chapter on *Macbeth*. The book was a revelation to me. I could not put the book down till I had read it all one morning, afternoon, and early evening on a lovely day in the Worcester College gardens. It articulated so beautifully so much that I had been fumbling both to think and say about literature. And then after reading Wimsatt and going through some of the works of Shakespeare with the incomparable tutelage of Christopher Ricks, I began in that first trimester at Oxford to believe that I might have something to say in this field someday, when I had the tools to say it.

And yet I still did not end up at Yale for my Ph.D. study, but at Cornell, simply because after seven years away, I could no longer bear the long stretches and distances away from family, home, and neighborhood. And once again, I was very lucky to be put immediately into the hands of Professors Arthur Mizener and M. H. Abrams, one a most distinguished practical, the other a theoretical critic, and both kind and considerate men.

I knew pretty well by then, in 1960, what I considered real criticism to be and also what I would consider a valid use of my time as a would-be critic to be. I had always Wimsatt's formulation in mind: "The verbal object and its analysis constitute the domain of literary criticism" and, it seemed to me, the literary works that most deserved close analysis would be those that were major achievements and at the same time not yet well analyzed. Professors Mizener, Robert M. Adams, and Stephen Whicher had introduced me for the first time in a rigorous way to the great Twentieth-century American poets and I was determined from that time on to explicate with as much precision and accuracy as I could manage the difficult texts of Wallace Stevens, Hart Crane, and Ezra Pound, who were at the time, it seemed to me, those least well understood. I was determined too to defend my positions on literary theory (or my distrust of theory) and literary criticism against the encroachments I then was aware of (largely the positions of Northrop Frye and Murray Kreiger). I have been largely at this job of work ever since, though the proliferation of literary theory from the Fifties till the present would force anyone but the most specialized scholar to back away from any pretense of a comprehensive overview. I make no such pretense here; I will sketch the scene and the major issues only as they have impinged personally on my own consciousness over the period.

Many things seemed patently obvious to me as a young reader in the Fifties (nothing, I have learned since, is obvious in Ontology): the literary text embodies the intentions of the author, as he makes those intentions known in the language and action of his text with more or less continuity--the creative act--and the reader responds to this communicative process with greater or less understanding--the critical act--while at the same time the same reader also makes decisions, valuations, of the extent to which the author's attitudes fit the values and the needs of the reader--the act of metacriticism. Most of what "critics", including philosophers and theoreticians and various sorts of ideologues, call criticism is in fact metacriticism.

These were the assumptions with which I read literature as a young man at Kenyon College with no time for theory. I had no real idea what critics belonged to what school. I had in fact no time for reading any critic thoroughly; either the critic helped me with the literary work I was reading or he did not. He had better help me in his early pages and he had better not expect me to pick up his book a second time on another author if he did not help me the first time with the first author. Good criticism was wherever you found it, from anyone who in the given pages of analysis was deeply engaged with the specific text and was struggling for precision and clarity concerning the attitudes and continuities of that text. As soon as the "critic" became more engaged with comparisons between a number of texts or the relationships of the text to ideologies extrinsic to the text, the criticism became metacriticism and of interest only to those who shared the metacritical values of the advocate.

I found great criticism in the pages of the older "Historicist" or "Philological" scholars such as W. P. Ker,

F. N. Robinson, E. K. Chambers, or J. R. R. Tolkien, and some weak, imprecise criticism from among those who were supposedly confronting Historicism with the "New Criticism," centered around Ransom and his *Review*. The Forties and Fifties were full of debates between Historical Scholarship or Philology and the New Criticism which focused on the integrity and quasi-autonomy of the literary work. It was (and still is) a debate full of red herrings, as has been the subsequent debates between later theoreticians and the by-now-old New Criticism.

It was the worst of red herrings to accuse Cleanth Brooks, the greatest of the New Critics, of being anti-historical or believing that a poem is autonomous i.e. ontologically self-sufficient, existing wholly in itself without any need for the understanding of its historical context. Brooks was a superb historical and textual scholar and never wrote that a literary work is insulated from historical context. And yet Murray Krieger (who taught at Kenyon for a while in the early Fifties) builds his remarks about Brooks in his very influential book *The New Apologists for Poetry* (1956) around this "organicist" thesis:

> ...the organicist must claim that the completely autonomous poetic context, one whose meaning is unique, *sui generis*, is also one that is utterly cut off from literary history as well as from literary criticism...It may be tempting to argue that the contextualist does not mean to maintain so

extreme, and thus so self-defeating, an organicism. But it is difficult to see how he can qualify it so long as he insists on the poem's autonomy, so long as he charges any translation, however cautious, of the terms in the context with "the heresy of paraphrase"...Yet this dead end of practical criticism seems hardly to be the aim of the more contextual of modern critics whose work has been distinguished by its painstaking detail of scrupulous verbal analysis...Yet respect for those sound aesthetic objectives that prompt a critic like Brooks does not alter the need to qualify the reckless implications of his theory (pp.136-8).

All of these "yets" and "buts" are testimony to Krieger's respect for Brooks's gifts as a critic, while Krieger's desire for total theoretical purity of ontological distinction makes him misrepresent Brooks's actual positions. The Romantic metaphor of a poem as living organism that can only be murdered by dissection is after all but a metaphor of an emotion, a metaphor which is useful only if not carried too far. While it is perhaps a truism that a complex poem can only be totally understood or explicated in its own words (that is, its context is what it is), one critical analysis can, certainly, as a limit (in the mathematical sense of limit, never reaching, though always getting closer), give a more precise sense of the meaning, or attitudes, of the poem than another. And this is all that criticism (using all the tools at its command, from history, philology, biography, etc.) can or ought to pretend to do: to help the reader to know a text as well as the author would have liked to have it known. To say that the context of a poem, like, say, Keats's *Grecian Urn*, is unique, unlike any other poem in the language, would also seem to be but a truism, but to say that it is therefore not susceptible to explication, partly through historical and other extrinsic data, is the furthest thing from Brooks's position, and it is reckless of Krieger to push the organicist metaphor to the extreme that he does. (Krieger admits to some distress in a later essay in *The Play and Place of Criticism*, 1967, pp.153-64, that his remarks, partially quoted above, may have been used by others to distort Brooks's position!).

I have written elsewhere (*The Rape of Cinderella, Essays in Literary Continuity*, 1970, and *Essays: Critical and Metacritical*, 1983) of the impact of Northrop Frye's *Anatomy of Criticism* (1957) on the literary world in general and on me at Kenyon in particular, and I will not repeat myself here. In any case, that impact and the limitations of Frye's positions on literary criticism have found their best assessments in Wimsatt's *Day of the Leopards* (1976). Frye's work is the fountainhead for a great number of "structuralist" approaches to literature. The consuming passion is to find some sort of structure or archetypal pattern which will contain or categorize (pigeonhole?) as large a number of literary works as possible. Comparative myth (as in Frye) or comparative folktale (as in Stith Thompson) are areas of study that have brought useful results to literary studies, but are tools towards precise criticism of individual works, not ends in themselves. So with "Comparative Literature" in general as a discipline--comparisons are useful but become odious if they tend towards the obliteration of the ways in which a given work is unique. What one finds in most structuralist writing on literature is a great deal of literary scholarship but not much real literary criticism, a great deal of relating of aspects of a work's thematics or techniques to those in a gathering of literary works, but not much close analysis of the work on its own terms.

But I want to move on to what I have felt over the past thirty years has become the greatest red herring of all in literary theory: the idea that the various modern encounters with Nominalism and Nihilism have shown that there is no fixed object of literary study, no text for analysis, at all.

Nihilism, the certainty that there is no "real" or "absolute" or "universal" basis for any belief in any order or direction or meaning in the universe and consequentially for any belief in any values, rights, or purpose in men's lives, has always been around in intellectual history as the dark side of the chiaroscuro in man's psyche, but it has gained the status as the dominant tonality in modern thought only in the post-Darwinian period. Nietzsche is the major philosopher of nihilism, but in his writings he always counterbalances his darker vision with the belief that man must have, therefore must create, values to live by. Thus Nietzsche has become the major prophet both for contemporary nihilists (via Sartre) and "fictionalists" (via Vaihinger and Unamuno). What needs to be realized however is that either position, or any other metacritical position, can be the basis for a literary work of continuity and coherence (see the "dialogue" between Krieger and Wimsatt in Chapter 14 of *The Play and Place of Criticism*, and my chapter on "Metacriticism" in *The Rape of Cinderella*).

A fashionable position of the Seventies and Eighties has been that since words have no relationship to the things of actuality ("Nominalism"), texts, which after all are made up of words, have no intrinsic meaning; texts are not unique entities which can be studied apart from other texts. Thus the "critic" can only funnel a given text through the literary and cultural associations of his own mind to create his own tapestry of language, one more text in the endless profusion of such from all the text-tapestry makers (writers and/or critics).

The position is inimical to precise literary criticism, almost as deadly as the laying on of, say, Freudian or Marxian or other supposedly archetypal patterns over specific literary works. As soon as one gives up the premise that there is a fixed object of study, fixed enough, that is, so that one statement is demonstrably more accurate about the object than another, then one has given up on the entire enterprise of analysis. There are no better or worse analyses, more or less precise or accurate analyses, and one critic is as good as another. This bogus idea may indeed be the real reason for the position being so fashionable. It has seemed to me that at the back of a great deal of "deconstructive" literary theorizing is the recognition by the theorist-critic somewhere along the line that he or she is not particularly gifted or interested in the close analysis of someone else's work, that what the given theorist-critic really enjoys is the free-flow of his own thoughts and associations, in which flow the stubborn literary text stands in the way like a stone. My own position is that ideologies are a dime a dozen and theories always on sale, whereas good criticism of another author's work cannot be produced, or bought or sold, on the cheap.

Wendell Harris, in his *Interpretive Acts* (1988), has argued persuasively the case for texts sufficiently fixed by the author's intentions, as he realizes them in the process of countless "speech-acts," and sufficiently communicated to the receptive reader to make "deconstruction" not only irrelevant but debilitating to literary criticism:

> What I wish to emphasize is...the contextual dependence of all discourse, and that this dependence cancels the free play of signs assumed for the purposes of deconstruction...Authors expect readers to interpret their works by searching for consonance and readers expect authors to expect them to do so. That consonance is never perfect

> is no more an argument against its use as a principle of interpretation than would be the contention that maps are pernicious because they can never be totally accurate...Interpretation requires reconstruction of the author's intention through awareness of the author's assumptions. Neither assumptions nor intentions change over time (though the difficulty in recovering them may)...what we seek is sufficient probability, sufficient unity, sufficient accuracy in interpretation.

Harris uses the word "interpretation" where I use the word "criticism," but to exactly the same purpose, that is, that, in his words, "an author's intended meaning *can* be understood with reasonable probability and accuracy."

Harris uses writings of J. Hillis Miller and Stanley Fish as representative of American deconstructive positions. He has this to say of Miller:

> Miller calls his commentary a reading' of the poem; the term is a useful one if understood in its most usual contemporary sense as an exercise of the critic's personal powers of association in the service of an externally derived theory...the strategy that produces Miller's reading is...the importation of analogues, parallels, or associations unauthorized by anything in the text, in effect denying that the structure of the text constitutes an internal context that limits possible meanings and relationships.

The emphasis throughout Harris's important work is properly on the limits of interpretation imposed by context, whereas the deconstructive theory is that the indeterminacy of all language and thought inevitably leads to an indeterminacy of both intention and interpretation, which leads to the by-now inevitable indeterminacy of any given text, which dissolved text then flows into the vast river of intertextuality and ends in the lifeless ocean of the *mise en abysme*, "the infinite regress of interpretation".

This gambit of there being no text to analyze is central to the deconstructive game, at least as played in America. I came to Stanley Fish's *Is There a Text in This Class?* (1980) with special interest because the four lectures which end the book were delivered at Kenyon College, about 40 years after the founding of the *Review* by Ransom. There is very little literary criticism in these lectures; the strategy of argumentation is to demonstrate the wide variability of interpretation to which short sentences or passages are susceptible. It is precisely Wendell Harris's main point that it is only in extended contexts that the limits of interpretation are provided by which the intended meanings of the author can be elicited:

> ...in the case of a single sentence interpretation involves discovering the consistency of that sentence with the external contextual dimensions, in the case of extended discourse we must seek interpretations that will be consistent as well with

> the...equivalents of these to which the text or utterance gives rise.

The "external contextual dimensions" are all of the elements that make up a "cultural grammar" (the term is Charles Altieri's), the background information an author could assume would be known by his contemporary readers. The author then proceeds to create a text which gives rise to internal relationships and meanings which limit free interpretation. Articulating these meanings as precisely as possible is what I have always defined as criticism.

Fish would have it that readers of various metacritical persuasions can only read someone else's text from their own vantage point:

> Interpretive communities are made up of those who share interpretive strategies not for reading (in the conventional sense) but for writing texts, for constituting their properties and assigning their intentions.

Christopher Ricks asks regarding this passage (in the *London Review of Books*, April 16, 1981), "Where does this leave writers, the original writers? Nowhere." For Fish, "criticism" inexorably lays bare the intentions and beliefs not of the author but of the critic and those who share his intentions and beliefs. For me, what is often called criticism does just what Fish says it does, but should be called metacriticism, and the term criticism saved for the process Fish seems to feel is impossible, the articulating as precisely as possible the meaning, the intentions and beliefs, of the author.

The "interpretive community" that every author seeks is the sum total of readers of the present and future who are willing to "suspend disbelief" for a while and live in the author's created world, adopt his "cultural grammar" and his beliefs, strive to understand his intentions and play by his rules. All other "interpretive communities" are not trying to be readers (in the only sense that matters to the author), but metacritics, using the author's text for their own games, played by their own rules. My view is that there are at any given time many readers of the first sort, and that from among this group come the true critics of a given work. There will always be far fewer true critics than true readers; many will not bother, having other things to do; many will simply not be articulate enough. One can feel the greatness of an author like, say, Cervantes, without having the training and the terms to articulate that sense of greatness.

The deconstructionist's game is a quite serious one. They are committed in a programmatic way, as Geoffrey Hartman states it, "to expunge divinity" from every sacred text (*Easy Pieces*, 1985, p.204). All God-centered literature must be decentered; there are no universal or absolute truths, and literature that posits absolutes is simply fantasy that cannot, to that extent, be taken seriously. This is a metacritical position, one which would devalue ("transvalue" is the word often used) a great part of the world's literature, which is the metacritic's prerogative, but it is not criticism. One is not reading a text by pointing out that since it deals with universals it is false, or that since words are inherently ambiguous, indeterminate in meaning, any given text can be shown to plausibly mean (to *really* mean?) the opposite of what it says it means. But this is in fact the deconstructive methodology (a variation on the Freudian "latent" vs. "manifest" content gambit); this is what Hartman means by his astounding statement in his *Criticism in the Wilderness*, 1980, that "we have perfected ...the technique of close reading". I do not believe it for a moment. There is no theoretical position--including the deconstructive--that is going to guarantee good criticism. Only sensitivity, close scrutiny and a talent for articulating precisely the central attitudes of a unique context is going to give us good criticism. One cannot will to be a good critic simply by having what one considers the right metaphysic, or the right literary theory. The deconstructive reader, like any sort of reader, must still return to the humbling but all-important job of the true critic, and no smoke-screen about the indeterminacy of language or the artistic text is going to hide a poor reading of a poorly understood text.

I have had occasion recently to review the late Italo Calvino's *The Uses of Literature* (1986). I already had great respect for his *Italian Folktales* (below p. 129), and found in this series of essays written between 1966 and 1982 a most interesting shift in Calvino's thinking, reflecting his growing dissatisfaction with the literary situation of his time. This is Calvino writing in the mid-Sixties:

> In Literature the writer is now aware of a bookshelf on which pride of place is held by the disciplines capable of breaking down the fact of literature into its primary elements and motivations, the disciplines of analysis and dissection (linguistics, information theory, analytical philosophy, sociology, anthropology, a new use of psychoanalysis, a new use of Marxism). To this library of multiple specializations we tend not so much to add a library shelf as to question its right to be there at all: literature today survives above all by denying itself.

By the mid-Seventies, we find a Calvino largely disenchanted with the hopes of the previous decade:

> [that] the dismantling of the work of literature might open the way toward a new evaluation and a new structuring. And what came of it? Nothing-- or exactly the opposite of what might have been hoped for...

And by 1981, Calvino wonders if the contemporary "critical" movements do not indicate a period of creative malaise:

> One might even say that storytelling is at one and the same time reaching the nadir of its eclipse in creative texts and the zenith of critical and analytical interest in it.

In these essays, then, we have the drama of a creative writer who, finally, after a long tour of the European (and, by extension, American) intellectual and critical scene, returns to his real home in his imagination:

> Any result attained by literature, as long as it is stringent and rigorous, may be considered firm ground for all practical activities for anyone who aspires to the construction of a mental order solid and complex enough to contain the disorder of the world within itself.

This sounds much like Wallace Stevens, who had indeed emerged as the major intellectual voice among the great Twentieth-century poets in the years since I had first read him and felt that he was the poet most worthy of, and most in need of, close analysis. The choice Calvino made is really the choice between the deconstructive nihilism grounded in one aspect of Nietzsche's thought and the philosophy of As If grounded in the other. One creates an order in which to live in defense against the disorder of reality because one must, because, as Wallace Stevens says in "Credences of Summer," "It was difficult to sing in face of the object." Stevens says in his "To the One of Fictive Music" to his "interior paramour," she who continues to sing despite the dismalness of objective reality, "Unreal, give back to us what once you gave:/ The imagination that we spurned and crave."

I would suggest (have suggested in my previous writings) that this is a better line to follow than the deconstructive, nihilistic line. The irrepressible desire for stability of values and the impossibility of any philosophic grounding of such values generates in Stevens and in many other modern thinkers a lauding of the imagination which can create the blessed myths, rituals, traditions, codes, within which a society or an individual might flourish. Though they seem so very different, both the archetypalist and the nihilist would attempt to discredit the value of such local orders, an achieved construct or context in either society or art. The one would tell the writer of *Jonah* that all enclosures, ship, whale, or water, are really the womb to which he wishes to return. The other would tell my mother that the lettuce leaf ought not to be seen as part of the divine, which doesn't exist.

We will always need a Wimsatt to tell both the archetypalist and the deconstructionist that the poet claims for a symbol "only the correctness of his momentary context," where the symbol can be divine or not, as the author wills, or a Wendell Harris to tell them that a symbol "can be recognized only in context," where it means only what it means in that context.

There will always be "critics" (Harold Bloom comes first to mind) anxious to subsume a given literary text into a larger system, willing to quash the actual tonality of a given work to squash it into the given thesis. But there will always also be the countervailing current, those who respect the unique literary context (Cleanth Brooks, of course, comes first to mind, but also, say, just to run up a list, R. P. Blackmur, Erich Auerbach, Kenneth Burke, Randall Jarrell, Harry Levin, Eric Bentley, Hugh Kenner, M. L. Rosenthal, Frank Kermode, Richard Ellmann, R. W. B. Lewis, Arthur Mizener, and Christopher Ricks) and the unique cultural context from which it comes, be it Dante's Tuscany, Cervantes's La Mancha, William Carlos Williams's Paterson, or even a little hill town in Lebanon at the turn of the century, or in Upstate New York in the mid-Fifties.

My own belief is that it is these latter sort of critics that deserve the name (call it New, or Contextual, or whatever), that they practice a lesser art which is yet an art, and that their usefulness and pleasure will outlive their generations and be useful and pleasing to generations after them (cf. Rene Wellek's closing remarks on the New Criticism in *Critical Inquiry*, Summer 1978). I cannot say the same for the various archetypalists and deconstructionists, who have for the last generation been writing so many premature obituaries for the other truer sort of critic.

Chapter Two

The Radiant Core: Family, Village, Neighborhood and Region in Literature.

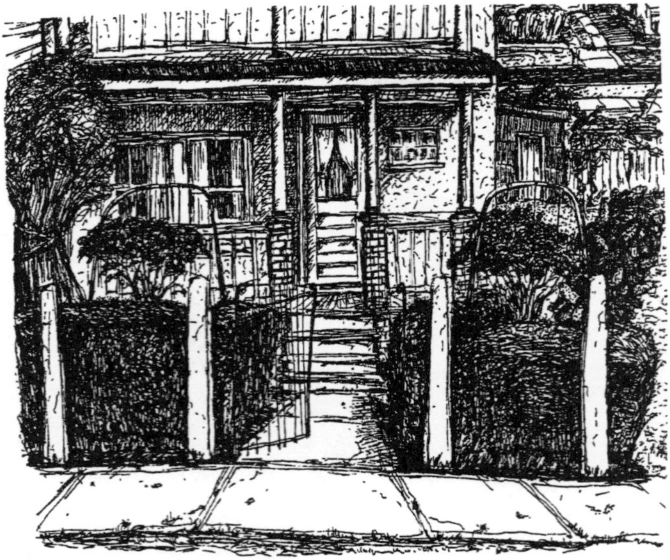

The roots of this essay certainly go back to my own experiences with family, neighborhood and region, to growing up Lebanese-American in an Italian-American neighborhood in the Upstate New York city of Utica. At age 64, I still live in the house in which I was born, walk the same streets, visit many of the same families, observe and feel the rhythms of birth, growth, maturity, decay and death in the families in the houses, in the gardens outside, and in the neighborhood. I am also a part of a region, and study and love its mythologies. I teach literature at a local college and feel, when I am researching, teaching, and writing about great works of literature and their social contexts, as if I am a citizen of the world, part of an international community of sympathetic, sensitive souls who think and feel as I do. I am also quite aware that in fact in that larger intellectual world many, if not most, do not think and feel as I do. This is always a surprising lesson, though one learned every day, if not every hour.

As I grew up loving the "stories" told to me by my parents and their generation and by those immigrant Italian neighbors of mine, and at the same time loving some of the major works of Western Literature (I remember especially being totally taken at age seventeen by Shakespeare's *King Lear*, Dostoyevski's

Brothers Karamazov and Tolstoy's *War and Peace*), I came to the belief that great literature, whether of the folk or of a supreme artist, is the best, the most complete and satisfying, re-creation of a precious social context, and also conversely (and more controversially), that the most enduring values expressed in great literature revolve around the joys of a given region and its cultures of family, village and neighborhood. It is this last proposition that might seem dubious to many readers and so the one I would like to give sufficient demonstration here to at least have the case presented.

We are in a time of anarchy and bewilderment concerning values, certainly including the values of familialism and localism. Many of my friends and colleagues in the '50's and '60's, largely children of immigrant parents, felt that they would be vulnerable to losing their hard-won status, socially or professionally, if they emphasized their ethnic, family, neighborhood or local roots, that these were things to be put behind one, things to be vaguely ashamed of. I never accepted such a position, though it probably was the right one for constructing a career at that time. And I certainly felt that the literature that I loved, both ancient and modern, counseled no such view of life.

The '70's saw some vigorous rebuttals of the anti-family and anti-localism positions from various quarters. Robert Nisbet for example argues in the concluding chapter of his *Twilight* of *Authority* (1975) for the "recovery" of "pluralism," "kinship," and "localism":

> Family has been more than the nidus of cohesion and of continuity; it has been visibly the source of themes in ethics, literature, and art which have been among the very brightest and most durable in the history of civilization...It should be obvious that family, not the individual, is the real molecule of society, the key link of the social chain of being...Along with the apparent beginnings of a renascence of the kinship tie are those of revival of the sense of locality and neighborhood. There is, of course, close affinity between the two types of social attachment, and there has been ever since the local community came into being...
> (pp. 254, 260)

Michael Novak in an article, "The Family Out of Favor," in *Harper's* (April, 1976):

> The role of a father, a mother, and of children with respect to them, is the absolutely critical center of social force. Even when poverty and disorientation strike, as over the generations they so often do, it is family strength that most defends individuals against alienation, lassitude, or despair...The family is the primary teacher of moral development. In the struggles and conflicts of marital life, husbands and wives learn the

realism and adult practicalities of love. Through the love, stability, discipline, and laughter of parents and siblings, children learn that reality accepts them, welcomes them, invites their willingness to take risks. The family nourishes "basic trust." From this spring creativity, psychic energy, social dynamism. If infants are injured here, not all the institutions of society can put them back together.

Christopher Lasch in his *Haven in a Heartless World: The Family Besieged* (1979):

> An understanding of the impact of the family on personality, and of the political implications of recent changes...makes it impossible any longer to equate defense of the nuclear family with reactionary politics or criticism of it with radicalism. Many radicals in the seventies have rediscovered the importance of family ties. (p. xv)

I do not intend this essay as a sociological, political, or religious tract, though no one's metacriticism of life is absent from anything he writes, but to demonstrate the profound strain of familialism and localism in some major literary works (those that I am wont to teach) from the earliest times to the present. Where then this might lead the reader is up to the reader. A modest theoretical underpinning for the subject at hand might however be supplied from Charles Horton Cooley's *Social Organization (1916)* and his definition of "human nature":

> The view here maintained is that human nature is not something existing separately in the individual...It is the nature which is developed and expressed in those simple, face-to-face groups that are somewhat alike in all societies; groups of the family...and the neighborhood. In the essential similarity of these is to be found the basis, in experience, for similar ideas and sentiments in the human mind. In these, everywhere, human nature comes into existence. Man does not have it at birth; he cannot acquire it except through fellowship and it decays in isolation...What kind or degree of association is required to develop it? Evidently nothing elaborate, because elaborate phases of society are transient and diverse, while human nature is comparatively stable and universal. In short the family and neighborhood life is essential to its genesis and nothing more is... (pp. 29, 31)

◆

The roots of Western Civilization are in the early Hellenic and Hebraic traditions. So says Matthew Arnold in *Culture and Anarchy* (1869), where he compares and contrasts the two traditions (the Hellenic clearly more to his liking), an analysis brilliantly carried on and refined by Erich Auerbach in the opening chapter of *Mimesis* (1946). A few substantial quotations from the *Odyssey* in the magnificent translation of the late Robert Fitzgerald can serve as paradigmatic for the Homeric sense of family:

> "Son of Laertes, versatile Odysseus,
> after these years with me, you still desire
> your old home? Even so, I wish you well.
> If you could see it all, before you go-
> all the adversity you face at sea-
> you would stay here, and guard this house, and be
> immortal-though you wanted her forever,
> that bride for whom you pine each day.
> Can I be less desirable than she is?
> Less interesting? Less beautiful? Can mortals
> compare with goddesses in grace and form?"
>
> To this the strategist Odysseus answered:
>
> "My lady goddess, here is no cause for anger.
> My quiet Penelope-how well I know-
> would seem a shade before your majesty,
> death and old age being unknown to you,
> while she must die. Yet, it is true, each day
> I long for home, long for the sight of home.
> If any god has marked me out again
> for shipwreck, my tough heart can undergo it.
> What hardship have I not long since endured
> at sea, in battle! Let the trial come.
>
> (5:203-224)

Home and wife (and elsewhere, son, mother, and father) are valued more than the gift of immortal life and youth with the goddess Kalypso. It is an awe-inspiring moment in the *Odyssey*. Of course we realize that Homer's audience has never had such a choice, but the moment speaks eloquently of the values Homer and his listeners wished to project to themselves.

Later Odysseus meets his mother in the Land of the Shades and in an intensely moving episode she says to him

>   your father
> is country bound and comes to town no more.
> He owns no bedding, rugs, or fleecy mantles,
> but lies down, winter nights, among the slaves,
> rolled in old cloaks for cover, near the embers.
> Or when the heat comes at the end of summer,
> the fallen leaves, all round his vineyard plot,
> heaped into windrows, make his lowly bed.
> He lies now even so, with aching heart,
> and longs for your return, while age comes on him.
> So I, too, pined away, so doom befell me,
> not that the keen-eyed huntress with her shafts
> had marked me down and shot to kill me; not
> that illness overtook me—no true illness
> wasting the body to undo the spirit;
> only my loneliness for you, Odysseus,
> for your kind heart and counsel, gentle Odysseus,
> took my own life away.'

> I bit my lip,
> rising perplexed, with longing to embrace her,
> and tried three times, putting my arms around her,
> but she went sifting through my hands, impalpable
> as shadows are, and wavering like a dream.
> Now this embittered all the pain I bore,
> and I cried in the darkness:
>
> 'O my mother,
> will you not stay, be still, here in my arms,
> may we not, in this place of Death, as well,
> hold one another, touch with love, and taste
> salt tears' relief, the twinge of welling tears?
> (11:183-211)

Such longing of parents for children, of children for parents, is reiterated throughout the Odyssey:

Odysseus reunited with his son Telemachus:

> "I am that father whom your boyhood lacked
> and suffered pain for lack of. I am he."
>
> Held back too long, the tears ran down his cheeks
> as he embraced his son...
> Telemakhos began to weep. Salt tears
> rose from the wells of longing in both men
> (16:187-191, 218-19)

And later, Odysseus reunited with his wife, Penelope:

> Now from his breast into his eyes the ache
> of longing mounted, and he wept at last,
> his dear wife, clear and faithful, in his arms,
> longed for
>   as the sunwarmed earth is longed for by a swimmer
> spent in rough water where his ship went down
> under Poseidon's blows, gale winds and tons of sea.
>   (23:230-36)

This longing, clearly inclusive of sexual longing, but encompassing longing also and especially for family, home and region, is what is understood as "love" by Homer and his audience. These longings, these values, are what I recognize as my longings, my values, and what I find I cannot help but expect (mistakenly) to be everyone's values. I still remember vividly the bafflement and irritation I felt in my undergraduate years at first reading the opening chapter of C. S. Lewis's *Allegory of Love (1936)*. I much respected Lewis's *English Literature in the 16th Century* and knew of his world reputation, and yet I found him here denigrating the power and integrity of "love" in the ancient world:

> There can be no mistake about the novelty of romantic love: our only difficulty is to imagine in all its bareness the mental world that existed before its coming...We must conceive a world emptied of that ideal of `happiness'-a happiness grounded on successful romantic love-which still

supplies the motive of our popular fiction. In ancient literature love seldom rises above the levels of merry sensuality or domestic comfort...we find the comfort and utility of a good wife acknowledged: Odysseus loves Penelope as he loves the rest of his home and possessions...(p.4)

The chapter reads, I would submit, as coming from one who has a grudge against "love" in any sense of the word except that of Christian love for God. He defines "Courtly Love" as compounded of "Humility, Courtesy, Adultery, and the Religion of Love" (p. 12), and he considers these attitudes as both endemic to "romantic love" over the past 1000 years and largely unhealthy for the soul. Be that as it may, I consider the "Homeric" attitudes toward "love" as both healthy and pervasive over the past 3-4000 years in the West (and, one might say, the East, v. Carle C. Zimmerman's comprehensive *Family and Civilization)*.

Homer's aim in the *Odyssey* is not only to tell the tales of the tribe with respect to heroes and monsters (Books 9-12), but to affirm a rich context of social values, the "laws and manners of old time," which include hospitality to "strangers and beggars," who "come from Zeus" (Books 1-4 & 13-24). It has been fashionable to see Books 9-12 as the true glory of the Odyssey, the opening books as preliminary to them, and the succeeding books as a long trailing-off in quality and pertinence. Such a view ignores Homer's clear intent to dramatize a social ethos. Telemachus is Homer's model of the dutiful son: having never seen his father, he tells a friend "I wish at least I had some happy man/as father, growing old in his own house" (1:217-18). Earlier he had come "straight to the door...irked with himself/to think a visitor had been kept there waiting" (1:117-18). He respectfully addresses the loyal swineherd Eumaios as "Uncle." To Penelope her son Telemachus is "more sweet to me than sunlight" (17:45). Nestor's family, the relationships between himself, his wife, and his sons, is held up by Homer and by Menelaos (4:207-9) as an example of "true felicity." Alkinoos's wife, Arêtê, is a model of an ideal matriarch, bearing little resemblance to C. S. Lewis's woman of ancient times (*op. cit.* p. 6) who would have been "ordered out of the room before the serious conversation about books, or politics, or family affairs began":

> When she grew up, Alkínoös married her
> and holds her dear. No lady in the world,
> no other mistress of a man's household,
> is honored as our mistress is, and loved,
> by her own children, by Alkínoös,
> and by the people. When she walks the town
> they murmur and gaze, as though she were a goddess.
> No grace or wisdom fails in her; indeed
> just men in quarrels come to her for equity.
>
> (7: 63-71)

I see the Lebanese mother and the Italian mother of East Utica in Arêtê. I walk the halls of Nestor, or Alkínoös, or Odysseus, with familiarity in my imagination, and wonder what the devil C. S. Lewis is talking about.

◆

The *Old Testament*, as a sacred anthology compiled of many authors and using oral traditions of over more than a thousand year period, is intrinsically more difficult to speak about with respect to any limited theme or subject like Family or Localism. The focus of the *Old Testament* on the worship of and obedience to the One God renders, of course, all other loyalties, loves, and devotions secondary. Thus Auerbach, in defining the core sense of reality for the Hebrews in *Mimesis*, chooses the scene of Abraham willing to sacrifice his beloved son Isaac to the will of Jehovah. (Arnold had defined Hebraism as a desire for the "will of God" and a "strictness of conscience," as contrasted to the "unimpeded play of thought" and the "spontaneity of consciousness" of the early Hellenic spirit.) The difficulties are compounded by the fact that the *Old Testament* stories are so often collages by various narrators from different time periods with differing points of view on crucial issues: the worship of local gods at high places or in sacred groves or of the One God on Mt. Zion; the proper relationships with the indigenous Canaanite culture;

the desirability of a tribal, or national, or international focus. And yet for all of these difficulties, I have always felt the presence of Familialism and Localism as values of great force throughout the *Old Testament*, if only and at times as mighty competitor to the dominant force of devotion to God only.

We can, for instance, imagine the early Hebrew audience's deep distress at the Lord's demand that Abraham sacrifice his son, as that which is dearest to him. The deepest chords are apparently struck in the Hebrew consciousness by King David weeping over the death of his infant son, taken away by God as punishment for the King's adultery with Bathsheba, and then later by the King's tears at the news of the death of Absalom, the favored illegitimate son, who had led a rebellion against his father. Similarly Joseph, the favored son of Jacob, weeps at the reunion with his half-brothers, though they, in their jealousy, had sold him into exile. Again, he weeps at the sight of his full brother, the faultless Benjamin:

> And Joseph made haste; for his bowels did yearn upon his brother: and he sought where to weep; and he entered into his chamber, and wept there. And he washed his face, and went out, and refrained himself...

Jacob mourns in the manner of King David at the news of the young Joseph's supposed death:

And Jacob rent his clothes, and put sackcloth upon his loins, and mourned for his son many days. And all his sons and all his daughters rose up to comfort him; but he refused to be comforted; and he said, For I will go down into the grave unto my son mourning. Thus his father wept for him...

Jacob laments later when the life of Benjamin is in danger: "...and God Almighty give you mercy before the man [Joseph], that he may send away... Benjamin. If I be bereaved of my children, I am bereaved." The brothers tell Joseph that "the lad cannot leave his father: for if he should leave his father, his father would die." The Joseph story makes the brothers' early treachery a manifestation of God's Will to save his People, and the happy ending is expressed by Joseph in these terms:

...go up to my father, and say unto him, Thus saith thy son Joseph, God hath made me lord of all Egypt: come down unto me, tarry not: and thou shalt dwell in the land of Goshen, and thou shalt be near unto me, thou, and thy children, and thy children's children...

This intensity of family feeling is dramatized in the Joseph story of fathers and sons and brothers, but elsewhere can be seen the strength of women in the Hebrew family. The following is from the *Book of Proverbs*:

> Who can find a virtuous woman? for her price is far above rubies.
> The heart of her husband doth safely trust in her...
> She considereth a field, and buyeth it: with the fruit of her hands she planteth a vineyard.
> She girdeth her loins with strength, and strengtheneth her arms.
> She perceiveth that her merchandise is good: her candle goeth not out by night...
> She stretcheth out her hand to the poor; yea she reacheth forth her hands to the needy...
> Strength and honour are her clothing; and she shall rejoice in time to come.
> She openeth her mouth with wisdom; and in her tongue is the law of kindness.
> She looketh well to the ways of her household, and eateth not the bread of idleness.
> Her children arise up, and call her blessed; her husband also, and he praiseth her... (31: 10-28)

Witness also the relationship of Abraham and Sarah ("And Sarah died... and Abraham came to mourn for Sarah, and to weep for her"), of Isaac and Rebekah ("And Isaac brought her into his mother Sarah's tent, and took Rebekah, and she became his wife; and he loved her: and Isaac was comforted after his mother's death"), of Jacob and Rachel ("And Jacob served seven years for Rachel; and they seemed unto him but a few days, for the love he had to her").

Admittedly, however, many of the relationships in

the *Old Testament* which are at times idyllic are at other times stormy, as the various narrators or compilers attempt to telescope through parable or allegory centuries of oral tradition concerning tribal movements and mores, complicated by the institutions of polygamy and concubinage and by conflicting attitudes on the part of narrators and compilers concerning the "right" sort of marriage. And certainly one selects from the mass of this material those moments, those vignettes, which exhibit what one is trying to demonstrate. Such difficulties keep recurring. Throughout the *Old Testament* runs the conflict between those authors for whom marriage between Jew and Non-Jew is an abomination in the sight of God and those for whom Jehovah as God of both Jew and Gentile alike will, under proper conditions, condone such marriages. The author of the *Book of Ruth* accepts a woman of Moab as King David's ancestor, as Ruth accepts unconditionally the family and traditions of her late husband. One presumes that King Solomon, as supreme politician of empire, knew exactly what he was doing in amassing 700 wives and 300 concubines from all of the ethnic and religious groups of the ancient Near East and in setting up altars to all of the gods of place of his neighbors. But at least one of the compilers of the Solomon stories finds in such behavior and Jehovah's displeasure in it the root cause of the ultimate fall of the Jewish State. Moses himself could not keep his people from worshiping the Baal and Astarte figures of the Canaanites; The Books of *Judges, Samuel* and *Kings* are replete with the condemnations of the constant falling away of the Hebrew peoples from the One God who must be worshipped at Mount Zion to the worship of the various Semitic gods of place at ancient high places or sacred groves throughout Canaan, Judea, Samaria, Philistia, and beyond. The various compilers of the *Old Testament* materials thus bear indirect testimony to the enormous pull of place, and pluralism, as well as familialism, in opposition to the pulls of exclusivism, of focus only on God's Will and only as it is understood at Mount Zion.

The sanctification of place apparently runs deep in the human heart, almost as deep as that of family. We Americans make semi-sacred a mountain in the Catskills by invoking the Presence of Rip Van Winkle. There is hardly a place in ancient Canaan, Israel, or Philistia that has not been sanctified by the human spirit and its religious imagination. It would seem that we go somewhat against the human grain when we try to take away this sacred feeling for place and presences. It is perhaps as Ezra Pound (admittedly a "difficult individual") said in various places in his *Cantos*, "Aram vult nemus" - "the grove needs an altar," "and all gates are holy," "vigor, quietude are of place," and "filiality and fraternity are the root...of the process." The intensity of devotion to place, to region, and filiality is to be sure tearing up the present Near East in the region of the *Old Testament*. Such intensity admittedly can generate the obverse of the feelings which I am advocating and which I feel much great literature illuminates. All good things have their tragic obverse. Can we retain the good and reject the bad? That is the reader's assignment, and the world's.

The *Psalms* and the *Song of Songs* beautifully evoke the local landscapes of the *Old Testament* region. Especially delightful for me are the references to the hills and streams, flowers, gardens, vineyards, and the cedar groves of Lebanon, as these are the subjects of the folk poetry that my mother and father and their peers used to sing in our living room. The love poetry of the *Songs* constitute an anthology typical of ancient Near Eastern secular poetry. Many of the songs of and to the bride are also compliments to family:

> Thou hast ravished my heart, my sister, my spouse; thou hast ravished my heart with one of thine eyes, with one chain of thy neck.
> How fair is thy love, my sister, my spouse! how much better is thy love than wine! and the smell of thine ointments than all spices!
> Thy lips, O my spouse, drop as the honeycomb: honey and milk are under thy tongue; and the smell of thy garments is like the smell of Lebanon.
> A garden inclosed is my sister, my spouse; a spring shut up, a fountain sealed.

The figuration is of bride as sister, the spring not yet flowing as the bride's virginity, and marriage as a fenced garden of delights.

> We have a little sister, and she hath no breasts: what shall we do for our sister in the day when she shall be spoken for?
> If she be a wall, we will build upon her a palace of silver: and if she be a door, we will inclose her with boards of cedar.
> I am a wall, and my breasts like towers: then was I in his eyes as one that found favour.

The sister, who will someday be bride, accepts the metaphor of walled garden as virtue, and the open door as looseness, as invitation to the "foxes that spoil the vines."

The beautiful, virginal, Rebekah dutifully brought her pitcher to the well of Ur and hospitably gave water and lodging to the servants of Isaac. This charming, idyllic moment (*Genesis* 24) distills the village dream of the ancient world: the right place, the right circumstances, and the right behavior.

Equally idyllic is the evocation of the sacred village well in Book 17 of the Odyssey:

> Down by the stony trail they made their way
> as far as Clearwater, not far from town-
> a spring house where the people filled their jars.
> Ithakos, Neritos, and Polyktor built it,
> and round it on the humid ground a grove,

> a circular wood of poplars grew. Ice cold
> in runnels from a high rock ran the spring,
> and over it there stood an altar stone
> to the cool nymphs, where all men going by
> laid offerings. (11.207-16)

Odysseus kisses the ground of his native land when Pallas Athene clears the mist she had thrown about it:

> "Now I shall make you see the shape of Ithaka.
> Here is the cove the sea lord Phorkys owns,
> there is the olive spreading out her leaves
> over the inner bay, and there the cavern
> dusky and lovely, hallowed by the feet
> of those immortal girls, the Naiades-
> the same wide cave under whose vault you came
> to honor them with hekatombs-and there
> Mount Neion, with his forest on his back!"
>
> She had dispelled the mist, so all the island
> stood out clearly. Then indeed Odysseus'
> heart stirred with joy. He kissed the earth,
> and lifting up his hands prayed to the nymphs:
>
> "O slim shy Naiades, young maids of Zeus,
> I had not thought to see you ever again!"
> (13:341-55)

One sacramentalizes one's home and its local objects, no matter whether the gods or goddesses be there beyond the mists or not, whether the presences be of the place or only of the mind.

◆

King Oedipus, blind, exiled from Thebes and accompanied only by his daughter Antigone, comes in his old age to Colonus, outside of Athens, and addresses a stranger:

Oedipus:
What is this region that we two have entered?

Stranger:
As much as I can tell you, I will tell.
This country, all of it, is blessed ground;
The god Poseidon loves it; in it the firecarrier
Prometheus has his influence; in particular
That spot you rest on has been called this earth's
Doorsill of Brass, and buttress of great Athens.
All men of this land claim descent from him
Who is sculptured here: Colonus, master horseman,
And bear his name in common with their own.
That is this country, stranger: honored less
In histories than in the hearts of the people.
 Sophocles, *Oedipus at Colonus*
 trans. Robert Fitzgerald, (New York:
 Harcourt, Brace. Harvest Book, 1941, p. 85)

We have in this play Sophocles in his own old age explaining to his audience, the citizens of Athens, the rise of their city-state on the ashes of Thebes, another

Greek city-state. It was the will of the gods that this happen, and Oedipus knows now at the end of his life that he is their unhappy instrument. It is not the same vision of the will of God that we have in the Hebrew *Old Testament* (at least not till we come to the *Book of Job*), but the sense of an elected people and a sacred place is much the same. Sophocles, looking with the weight of years at the tragic scene of life. counsels submission to the inscrutable will of the gods, and for all of his respect for the Athenian state of the 5th century, considers as part of divine law one's obligations to family, and therefore obligations to family, and to the divine, as taking precedence over civil law. The filial devotion in *Oedipus at Colonus* is deep:

> Antigone: Lean your old body on my arm;
> It is I, who love you; let yourself down...
>
> Oedipus: My sweet children!
>
> Antigone: To our father, sweet indeed.
>
> Oedipus: My staff and my support!
>
> Antigone: And partners in sorrow.
>
> Oedipus: I have what is dearest to me in the world.
> To die, now, would not be so terrible,
> Since you are near me
> Press close to me, child,
> Be rooted in your father's arms

Oedipus's sons were ambitious and disobeyed their father; ultimately they kill one another. But Antigone loves her brothers and attempts to reconcile them to one another and to their father. It is hopeless, and Antigone laments:

> Who would not grieve for you,
> Sweet brother! You go with open eyes to death!...
> Then I am lost,
> If I must be deprived of you!

Oedipus's final words to Antigone and her sister Ismene are these:

> Children, this day your father is gone from you.
> All that was mine is gone. You shall no longer
> Bear the burden of taking care of me-
> I know it was hard, my children. -And yet one word
> Frees us of all the weight and pain of life:
> That word is love. Never shall you have more
> From any man than you have had from me.

Later, with father and both brothers dead, Antigone rouses her sister to her duty to disobey King Creon's "new law" forbidding the proper burial of their brother, who had been a traitor to Thebes:

> There it is,
> And now you can prove what you are:
> A true sister, or a traitor to your family.

And then in debate with King Creon:

> Antigone: All these men here would praise me
> Were their lips not frozen shut with fear of you...
>
> Creon: ...you honor a traitor as much as him.
>
> Antigone: His own brother, traitor or not, and equal in blood.
>
> Creon: He made war on his country...
>
> Antigone: Nevertheless, there are honors due all the dead.

Haimon, Creon's son and lover to Antigone, makes clear to his father (and the Greek audience) that the deepest feelings of the people are with Antigone:

> ...and I have heard them
> Muttering and whispering in the dark about this girl.
> They say no woman has ever, so unreasonably,
> Died so shameful a death for a generous act:
> "She covered her brother's body. Is this indecent?
> She kept him from dogs and vultures. Is this a crime?
> Death?-She should have all the honor that we can give her!"

Once again is demonstrated the pervasive force of family in the ancient world, and the force of love, *maugre* C. S. Lewis, properly defined. And as with Antigone, so with Virgil's Aeneas, as he leads father and son, and doomed wife, along with his household gods, out of the burning Troy, as he later gives up Dido, under obligation to his family and his gods. Virgil in the *Aeneid* gives dramatic intensity to the ideals of family as enunciated in Cicero's "Dream of Scipio." Sophocles, Cicero, Virgil, are all giving basically the same answer to the reiterated questions in the *Odyssey*, the questions that we still ask ourselves, "Who are you? Where do you come from? Where's your home and family?"

◆

"O Tuscan, who go living through this place
speaking so decorously, may it please you pause
a moment on your way, for by the grace

of that high speech in which I hear your birth,
I know you for a son of that noble city
which perhaps I vexed too much in my time on earth"...

And when I stood alone at the foot of the tomb,
the great soul stared almost contemptuously,
before he asked: "Of what line do you come?"
    (trans. John Ciardi, *The Inferno,* N.Y. New American Library, 1954)

Farinata degli Uberti addresses Dante in Canto 10 of *The Inferno* with essentially the same questions in the Homeric formula of some 2000 years earlier, save that Farinata has already caught the Florentine accent of the Tuscan dialect and the educated level of Dante's speech. Upon learning Dante's lineage, Farinata notes that Dante's clan were "bitter enemies... to me, to my father."

Throughout *The Inferno*, sinners and non-sinners alike are obsessed with one's clan and one's town; there is a steady stream of sometime savage, sometime sardonic or burlesque, denunciation and imprecation of the various cities and notable families of Tuscany and beyond. *The Inferno* has an intensely local and regional focus, as well as a universal and transcendental intention. The very worst effects of what is called "campanilismo," the caring only for what lies within hearing of the village's church bell, is demonstrated in *The Inferno*, but always as the dark side to the light and life which also flows from family and localism. Dante is clearly proud of being a Florentine for all of his deprecation of it and its citizens. He is in awe of Farinata as soldier and man of integrity though Farinata was a freethinker, punished in Hell as an heretic. Sharing the sepulchre with Farinata is Cavalcanti dei Cavalcanti, the cultured father of Guido Cavalcanti, poet and friend of Dante, who much influenced Dante's early lyrics. Burning in Hell for heresy, the father only wants news of his son, and swoons when he mistakenly thinks that his son is dead. It is much like the effect in the *Odyssey* where Akhilleus in the Land of the Shades, after complaining bitterly to Odysseus about the misery of existence in the Underworld, is temporarily solaced by news of the good repute of his living son. In the midst of the miseries of Hell, Dante's sinners are consistently concerned for what they cared about on earth: their families, their villages or towns, their being remembered, for better or worse, by their families and friends back in their regions. Dante himself feels great pain in Canto 29, when he is told by Virgil, after enquiring concerning his cousin, Geri del Bello, that del Bello had glowered at Dante for failing in the family obligation to take revenge for his murder. Dante accepts the vendetta obligation for family honor, even for a cousin in Hell for the sin of sowing discord.

Dante has the highest respect for Bertrand de Born, the Provencal poet, but will place him in Hell as a sower of family discord. De Born speaks to Dante holding his own head in his hand, decapitated justly, as de Born says himself, for setting

> son against father, father against son
> as Achitophel set Absalom and David;
> and since I parted those who should be one
> in duty and in love, I bear my brain
> divided from its source within this trunk,
> (Canto 28, 11.136-40)

And then in the most pathetic and celebrated vignette

in the *Inferno*, we have the ultimate symbol of filial love, when Ugolino's children offer themselves to their father, as they all lay starving locked in a tower:

> When a tiny ray leaked into that dark prison
> and I saw staring back from their four faces
> the terror and the wasting of my own,
>
> I bit my hands in helpless grief. And they,
> thinking I chewed myself for hunger, rose
> suddenly together. I heard them say:
>
> "Father, it would give us much less pain
> if you ate us"...   (Canto 33, 11.55-62)

To be sure, it was Ugolino's treachery and his treacherous friends that put him and his children in the tower in the first place, but no matter, whether through Abraham's piety or Ugolino's perfidy, the portrait of the child s trust in its father is inexpressibly tender.

◆

Chaucer's *Canterbury Tales* are suffused with the radiance of the sacred in the commonplace, the love of the local. The whole is embraced by a vision of life that found its prose formulation in Aristotle's *Metaphysics* and its quintessential poetic expression in the opening lines of Chaucer's *Prologue*:

Whan that April with his showres soote
The droughte of March hath perced to the roote,
And bathed every veine in swich licour,
Of which vertu engendred is the flowr;
Whan Zephyrus eek with his sweete breeth
Inspired hath in every holt and heeth
The tendre croppes, and the yonge sonne
Hath in the Ram his halve cours yronne,
And smale fowles maken melodye
That sleepen al the night with open ye-
So priketh hem Nature in hir corages-
Thanne longen folk to goon on pilgrimages.

The love of the feminine Earth by the masculine Rain, Wind, and Sun, the Love of the Creator implicit in the natural world ("so priketh hem Nature in hir corages"), has its fullest actualization in the religious instincts of mankind. All things in their places in the divine plan are intensely interesting to Chaucer, from the Pardoner's metaphysical bitterness to the hole in the door for the cat in the *Miller's Tale*. The reader is in the presence of a local world which seems totally realized in art; we have at least the illusion of being totally "at home" in Chaucer's London, observing satirically, for instance, the social-climbing Guildsmen and their assenting wives (*Prologue*, 11.363-380), or at court, assessing the squire, who "carf biforn his fader at the table" (1.100, an assessment which finally can only affirm his true filial devotion).

Most pertinent to our subject is Chaucer's magical evocations of village and country life. The Miller's coarse brutality is offset by a lyrical love for country things that is captivating, as in his description of Alison:

> She was ful more blisful on to see
> Than is the newe perejonette tree,
> And softer than the wolle is of a wether...
> But of hir song, it was as loud and yerne
> As any swalwe sitting on a berne.
> Therto she coude skippe and make game
> As any kide or calf folwing his dame.
> Hir mouth was sweete as bragot or the meeth,
> Or hoord of apples laid in hay or heeth.

The Miller is a master of the idioms of common life, with also an impeccable eye for village routine on the farm, in the church, the barber's chair, and at the blacksmith's. What he does not have is a moral vision of life beyond wine, women, and song, or any respect for the institutions of medieval society, all of which he feels are full of affectation merely.

What the Miller lacks is supplied with Chaucerian fulness in the Nun's Priest, who, while equally charmed by village life and equally aware of academic and aristocratic pretensions, affirms Christian charity and humility as the moral glory of God's design. The pretensions of court and of learning, both scientific and humanistic, are mocked through the hen and the cock and the fox, all acting like aristocrats in the barnyard chicken coop of the old peasant woman. The poor widow and her daughters control, of course, the chickens and the coop, and the Nun's Priest, through such a comic inversion, is genially noting to his audience that it is the peasantry, its family values, its labor, and its village rhythms that are enduring in human societies:

> A poore widwe somdeel stape in age
> Was whilom dwelling in a narwe cotage,
> Biside a grove, stonding in a dale:
> This widwe of which I telle you my tale,
> Sin thilke day that she was last a wif,
> In pacience ladde a ful simple lif.
> For litel was hir catel and hir rente,
> By housbondrye of swich as God hire sente
> She foond hirself and eek hir doughtren two.
> Three large sowes hadde she and namo,
> Three kin, and eek a sheep that highte Malle...
> No daintee morsel passed thurgh hir throte—
> Hir diete was accordant to hir cote.
> Repleccioun ne made hire nevere sik:
> Attempre diete was al hir physik,
> And exercise and hertes suffisaunce.

"Hertes suffisaunce" is likewise at the core of the encomium to the Plowman and his neighborliness in the *Prologue*:

> A trewe swinkere and a good was he,
> Living in pees and parfit charitee.
> God loved he best with al his hoole herte
> At alle times, though him gamed or smerte,
> And thanne his neighebor right as himselve.
> He wolde thresshe, and therto dike and delve,
> For Cristes sake, for every poore wight,
> Withouten hire, if it laye in his might.

As well as of his "brother," (blood brother? or, as with Saint Francis, a spiritual brother?), the Parson:

> ...a poore Person of a town,
> But riche he was of holy thought and werk.
> Benigne he was, and wonder diligent,
> And in adversitee ful pacient,
> ...rather wolde he yiven, out of doute,
> Unto his poore parisshens aboute
> Of his offring and eek of his substaunce.
> He coude in litel thing have suffisaunce.

These passages describing the Parson, Plowman, and the Poor Widow are, to be sure, panegyric, and do not have the Chaucerian irony that gives the *Canterbury Tales* its complexity. They are however at the emotional center of Chaucer's values, the home to which he can return after excursions, comic or tragic.

◆

At the center of Shakespeare's emotional life, I

would assert, are loves not much different from Chaucer's. With Shakespeare we have an unparalleled lyricism for the English countryside, which every reader has felt, and an equally compelling evocation of common life in the villages and the city. In *Henry IV, Pt. Two*, we hear of the early carousings of Falstaff in Gloustershire and experience them in his later life at the Boar's Head Tavern of Eastcheap in London in both Parts *One* and *Two*. Prince Hal on the tavern life:

> ...I do now remember the poor creature, small beer. But indeed these humble considerations make me out of love with my greatness.
> (II:2,11.10-12)

Falstaff on the memories of youth in Gloustershire: "We have heard the chimes at midnight, Master Shallow." (III:2,201). "The heart's all" says Davy, servant to Shallow, at a reunion in Gloustershire, and he is echoed by Master Silence: "now comes in the sweet o' th' night" (V:3,.29, 49). Sweet indeed are the evenings of Prince Hal and Falstaff in the neighborhood of Eastcheap. Wide of the mark, it seems to me, the critical assertions that Hal despises the tavern life and is simply dissembling in the scenes of that life. Prince Hal's father, Henry IV, is a dissembler, a cold, calculating, and quite unhappy man; Hotspur is a warm, impulsive, and unhappy man. Henry IV and Hotspur are two aristocrats who both feel a sense of dishonor; Hal is between, attracted more to Hotspur's ardour than to his father's cunning. But so poor are these aristocratic choices, the politics of war and treachery and so forth, that the tavern life, the neighborhood life of non-important people, the life that Sir John Falstaff chose long ago, has great attraction for the young Prince.

It would not be so attractive if Hal had a better father. Hamlet's dilemma would not be so pointed if he had a better mother; Lear's tragedy not so poignant had he two better daughters. As we move from the greatest of Shakespeare's history plays to the greatest of his tragedies, we find the much-noted "world-weariness" of the protagonists, the "weltschmertz" that almost overwhelms the tragic plays, deeply involved with issues of family. Hamlet feigns madness, Lear has bouts with madness, both driven by shock over and disillusionment with those closest to them.

Hamlet's first soliloquy:

> How weary, stale, flat, and unprofitable,
> Seem to me all the uses of this world!
> Fie on 't! ah fie! 'T is an unweeded garden,
> That grows to seed; things rank and gross in nature
> Possess it merely. That it should come thus!...
> O God! a beast, that wants discourse of reason,

> Would have mourn'd longer--married with my uncle,
> My father's brother, but no more like my father
> Than I to Hercules; within a month,
> Ere yet the salt of most unrighteous tears
> Had left the flushing in her galled eyes,
> She married. O, most wicked speed, to post
> With such dexterity to incestuous sheets!
> (I:2,.33-7, 50-7)

Lear on his daughters, Goneril and Regan:

> Filial ingratitude!
> Is it not as this mouth should tear this hand
> For lifting food to 't? But I will punish home.
> No, I will weep no more. In such a night
> To shut me out! Pour on; I will endure.
> In such a night as this! O Regan, Goneril!
> Your old kind father, whose frank heart gave all,-
> O, that way madness lies; let me shun that;
> No more of that.   (III:4,.15-23)

In the Shakespearean tragic vision, the true madness of humanity lies in its inhumanity and beastiality, especially when exhibited in the unnaturalness of family violence. Albany to his wife:

> O Goneril!
> You are not worth the dust which the rude wind
> Blows in your face. I fear your disposition.

> That nature, which contemns it origin,
> Cannot be bordered certain in itself.
> She that herself will sliver and disbranch
> From her material sap, perforce must wither
> And come to deadly use...
> Tigers, not daughters, what have you performed?
> A father, and a gracious aged man,
> Whose reverence even the head-lugged bear would lick,
> Most barbarous, most degenerate, have you madded...
> If that the heavens do not their visible spirits
> Send quickly down to tame these vile offenses,
> It will come,
> Humanity must perforce prey on itself,
> Like monsters of the deep.
> (IV:2,.31-35, 42-5, 48-52)

Hamlet has the love of Ophelia, Lear the love of his daughter Cordelia, but Hamlet is too sick at heart over his mother's disloyalty to accept Ophelia's love, and Lear is prevented by evil forces from having Cordelia's for very long. The world may be seen as either "goodly frame" or as "sterile promontory" (*Hamlet*, II:2); which view, comic or tragic, one has in Shakespeare, as in life, is often predicated on the strength of flow of the "material sap" through the branches of family.

◆

The essentially comic vision of Cervantes flows,

in the words of Erich Auerbach, from a "gaiety in the portrayal of everyday reality" (op.cit.p.358). That portrayal, in all of its "multifariousness," has as its moral and emotional center the village life of Cervante's time and place. And an exquisite village culture it is, rich in folk humor and proverbial wit and wisdom, charity, warmth, and neighborliness. Don Quixote was Alonso Quijano the Good in the years before he sallied forth, and as a man of gentleness and generosity he inspired the loyalty and devotion of all those around him in his village in the region of La Mancha: his niece, the housekeeper, the servant boy, the village curate, the barber, the scholar Sanson Carrasco, his neighbors Tomé Cecial and Pedro Alonso, and, of course, Sancho:

> I know that if I had good sense I'd have left my master long ago. But this is my luck, my misfortune, and I can't help following him. We're from the same village, I've eaten his bread, I like him very much, he's generous to me...and, above all, I'm loyal; and so it's impossible for anything to separate us except the pick and spade.
> (trans. Samuel Putnam, N.Y.
> The Viking Press, 1951, Pt.II:Ch.23)

Sancho strings village proverbs together much to the despair of Don Quixote, but to the delight of the reader and of Cervantes, who has the prodigious memory for folk literature that he gives to Sancho.

Quixote, after each series of adventures, returns to his home village, where those who love him will care for him, no matter how absurd his actions. And it is to the village culture that Cervantes keeps returning, as the haven of good sense and good feelings. Tome Cecial on family:

> "Really and truly, Sir Squire, ... I have made up my mind and resolved to have no more to do with the mad whims of these knights; I intend to retire to my village and bring up my little ones-I have three of them, and they are like oriental pearls." (II:13)

Sancho (speaking first to his grey donkey) on the rhythms of village life:

> "Come, comrade and friend," he said, "partner in all my troubles and hardships. When I was with you, I had no other care than that of mending your harness and feeding that little carcass of yours. Those for me were the happy hours, days, and years; but since leaving you and mounting the towers of ambition and pride, a thousand troubles, a thousand torments, and four thousand worries have entered my soul"...
> "Clear the way, gentlemen, and let me go back to my old freedom. Let me go look for my past life so that I may be resurrected from this present death. I was not born to be a governor or to

defend islands and cities from enemies that would attack them. I know more about plowing and digging and pruning vines that I do about the laws or the protection of islands and kingdoms. (II:53)

Here we have Pedro Alonso, Quixote's neighbor, as good Samaritan:

> The farmer was astounded at hearing all these absurdities, and after removing the knight's visor which had been battered to pieces by the blows it had received, the good man bathed the victim's face, only to discover, once the dust was off, that he knew him very well."...sinner that I am, cannot your Grace see that I am not Don Rodrigo de Narvaez nor the Marquis of Mantua, but Pedro Alonso, your neighbor? And your Grace is neither Baldwin nor Abindarraez but a respectable gentleman by the name of Senor Quijana." (I:5)

And Don Diego de Miranda as proper country gentleman:

> I spend my life with my wife and children and with my friends. ..."Sometimes...I dine with my friends and neighbors, and I often invite them to my house. My meals are wholesome and well prepared and there is always plenty to eat. I do not care for gossip, nor will I permit it in my presence. I am not lynx-eyed and do not pry into the lives and doings of others. I hear mass every

day and share my substance with the poor, but make no parade of my good works lest hypocrisy and vainglory, those enemies that so imperceptibly take possession of the most modest heart, should find their way into mine. I try to make peace between those who are at strife. (II:16)

Such a life would Don Quixote undoubtedly have led had he the wherewithal and had he not gone mad over the dubious heroics, the fustian and bombast of the Chivalric Epic. Quixote's actions are always admirable though consistently ineffectual. Cervantes' delicious sense of the absurd is everywhere evidenced as Quixote's unhinged idealism is confronted with the realities of his time, both harsh and sweet.

The peasant response to the realities, usually harsh, of its existence has consistently been to embrace the available joys of family and village culture. Among these are the humorous and satiric folk tale, where here, at least, the peasant is victorious. Sancho's tenure as Governor of Barataria "Island" is a series of comic triumphs of the folk imagination. Sancho tests the truthfulness of the prostitute who cried rape by calling for her purse to be snatched. As she fought like a tigress to keep her purse, so, Governor Sancho observes, she might have fought to keep her "virginity" (II:45). This is the stuff of folk tale, repeated and revised in oral transmission till it is used by a master like Cervantes, who clearly handles it with loving care. Similarly the tale of the farmer who petitions Sancho for a letter of recommendation between families for his grotesque son to marry the hideous daughter of a neighbor, as well as a gift of a dowry for the couple from the Governor (II:47). I need no dictionary of folk tale motifs to know that I have heard these stories in different frames, both from the Lebanese immigrants who used to come to our house for "evenings" long ago and from the immigrant Italian old man down the block who would call me up onto his porch to tell me "stories." Here is the "human nature" that Charles Horton Cooley speaks about as developed out of the similarity in most cultures of family and village life. Never has its comic aspects been better, more richly portrayed than in Cervantes.

◆

The influence of *Don Quixote* is pervasive in the literature of Eighteenth Century England, not from any sense of Quixote as isolated, tragic, existential hero, which view comes in with Romanticism in the Nineteenth Century, but from the human comedy, the gaiety, and warmth in the scenes of village life and life on the road. Fielding, Sterne, and Smollett, the great novelists of the period, for instance, are all professed disciples of Cervantes, sharing his penchant for burlesque satire and his love of the provincial.

Burlesque satire is the major mode, the great creative thrust of the period, and Jonathan Swift the greatest genius in the mode (with Pope and Gay not far behind). The satiric targets of Swift are those of inflation, pomposity and hypocrisy and, deeper, the pretensions of transcendental knowledge, of grand abstractions, philosophic systems, dogmatics of religion and science, and their sometime effects: war, empire, and colonialism. The values of Swift, the opposites to these evils, are with Swift, as with most satirists, not so often articulated as implied, but are those of local charity, intellectual humility, and the maintenance of what he calls the 'common forms':

> Then has this Madness been the Parent of all those mighty Revolutions, that have happened in Empire, in Philosophy, and in Religion. For, the Brain, in its natural Position and State of Serenity, disposeth its Owner to pass his Life in the common Forms, without any Thought of subduing Multitudes to his own Power, his Reasons or his Visions... *Tale of a Tub*, Sec IX

It is Lord Munodi ("Munodi": "I hate the world, "i.e., the world of power, from which he has resigned) who lives in the manner which Swift approves:

> ...in three Hours travelling, the Scene was wholly altered; we came into a most beautiful Country; Farmers Houses at small Distances, neatly built, the Fields enclosed, containing Vineyards, Corngrounds and Meadows. Neither do I remember

to have seen a more delightful Prospect. His Excellency observed my Countenance to clear up; he told me with a Sigh, that there his Estate began, and would continue the same till we should come to his House. That his Coutrymen ridiculed and despised him for managing his Affairs no better, and for setting so ill an Example to the kingdom... as for himself being not of an enterprizing Spirit, he was content to go on in the old forms.
Gulliver's Travels, Part 3, Ch. 4.

Munodi is but one representative in a long line of fundamentally benevolent, though sometimes eccentric or acerbic English gentlemen, all somewhat in the tradition of Don Alonso Quijano the Good who becomes Don Quixote the Mad. Addison and Steele's Sir Roger de Coverly, Fielding's Parson Adams and Squire Allworthy, Sterne's Uncle Toby, Goldsmith's Primrose and Hardcastle, and Smollett's Matthew Bramble, are all also proponents of Horace's *jucunda oblivia vitae* - the joys of the quiet, rural life. Matthew Bramble's letter of June 8th in *Humphry Clinker*, too long to quote in its entirety here, is classic of the view:

At Brambleton-hall, I have elbow-room within doors, and breathe a clear, elastic, salutary air--I enjoy refreshing sleep, which is never disturbed by horrid noise, nor interrupted, but in a-morning, by the sweet twitter of the martlet at my window-I

> drink the virgin lymph, pure and chrystalline as it gushes from the rock, or the sparkling beveridge, home-brewed from malt of my own making... my bread is sweet and nourishing, made from my own wheat, ground in my own mill, and baked in my own oven; my table is, on a great measure, furnished from my own ground...

Goldsmith's Parson Primrose:

> There was in fact nothing that could make us angry with the world or each other. We had an elegant house, situated in a fine country and a good neighbourhood. The year was spent in moral or rural amusements... We had no revolutions to fear, nor fatigues to undergo; all our adventures were by the fire-side, and all our migrations from the blue bed to the brown.
> *The Vicar of Wakefield*, Ch. 1.

And his Hardcastle:

> I love everything that's old: old friends, old times, old manners, old books, old wine; and, I believe, Dorothy, you'll own I have been pretty fond of an old wife.   *She Stoops to Conquer*, I:1

Hardcastle has prevailed upon his daughter Kate to wear a housewife's dress in the afternoons rather than the finery of the rich. He has a warm and intimate relationship with all of the servants of his estate which, however sentimentalized by Goldsmith, symbolizes a yearning for a social stability and cohesion that many of the period felt was being lost. The loss of aristocratic, yeoman, and peasant virtues is lamented throughout the period as an effect of the enormous growth of an urban, commercial, ultimately an industrial society:

> Sweet Auburn! loveliest village of the plain,
> Where health and plenty cheered the laboring swain...
> Dear lovely bowers of innocence and ease,
> Seats of my youth, when every sport could please,
> How often have I loitered o'er thy green,
> Where humble happiness endeared each scene;
> How often have I paused on every charm,
> The sheltered cot, the cultivated farm,
> The never-failing brook, the busy mill,
> The decent church that topped the neighboring hill...
>
> Sweet smiling village, loveliest of the lawn,
> Thy sports are fled, and all thy charms withdrawn...
> "The Deserted Village" (.1-12, 35-6)

Fielding's *Tom Jones* is the quintessential dramatization of a country culture that is still flourishing, symbolically presided over by the kindly Squire Allworthy, and an urban culture that is not, symbolized by the moral and physical decay in the ageing Lady Bellaston in London. Allworthy, to be sure, has the fault of a lack of insight into people, and Tom Jones the fault of youthful imprudence, but both have the inestimable gift of active benevolence, which for Fielding is the true definition of "love":

> There is in some (I believe in many) human breasts a kind and benevolent disposition, which is gratified by contributing to the happiness of others. That in this gratification alone, as in friendship, in parental and filial affection, as indeed in general philanthropy, there is a great and exquisite delight. That if we will not call such disposition love, we have no name for it.
> *Tom Jones*, Book VI, Ch. 1.

This definition of love is not essentially different from Homer's, (above, p) if we include hospitality under benevolence, and add the love of place, as with Odysseus' love for Ithaca, and Tom's for Somersetshire. There are admittedly flaws in the filial affections in *Tom Jones*: Bridget Allworthy, Tom's mother, both hides and compromises her affections; Squire Western's great love for his daughter Sophia is often spoilt by his tyrannical behavior. Likewise, in *Humphry Clinker*, the genuine affection of Matthew Bramble for his sister Tabitha, and hers for him, is often soured by her foolishness and his acerbity. Reverend Primrose, the Vicar of Wakefield, has a wife prone to vanities, but still, as he says,

"we loved each other tenderly, and our fondness increased with age...Sometimes...my wife and I would stroll down the sloping field, that was embellished with blue-bells and centaury, talk of our children with rapture, and enjoy the breeze that wafted both health and harmony."
(Chap.'s 1, 5)

"My father" in Sterne's *Tristram Shandy* is often lost in abstractions and is possessed of a dim-witted wife, yet his family feeling is real and affecting:

> My father, I believe, had the truest love and tenderness for my uncle Toby, that ever one brother bore towards another, and would have done any thing in nature, which one brother in reason could have desired of another, to have made my uncle Toby's heart easy in this, or any other point...
> Brother Toby, said he-I beg thy pardon;- forgive, I pray thee, this rash humour which my mother gave me.-My dear, dear brother, answered my uncle Toby, rising up by my father's help, say no more about it;-you are heartily welcome, had it been ten times as much, brother. But 'tis ungenerous, replied my father, to hurt any man;-a brother worse;-but to hurt a brother of such gentle manners,-so unprovoking,-and so unresenting;-'tis base:-By Heaven, 'tis cowardly.-You are heartily welcome, brother, quoth my uncle Toby,-had it been fifty times as much... (I:21, II: 12)

The scenes of brotherly affection combined with mutual noncomprehension in Shandy Hall are magical and wistful, the tragic story of the narrator as consumptive in love with life, life radiant with nuances of emotion and sense of place, deeply moving.

In the seventh book of *Tristram Shandy* and throughout the *Sentimental Journey*, we have Sterne knowing that he is dying, traveling in search of the core sentiments of human nature and finding them, symbolically, in the South of France among the peasantry.

> I could wish, continued I, to spy the nakedness of their hearts, and through the different disguises of customs, climates, and religion, find out what is good in them to fashion my own by-and therefore am I come...'tis a quiet journey of the heart in pursuit of Nature, and those affections which arise out of her, which make us love each other-and the world, better than we do.
> *A Sentimental Journey Through France and Italy* (Book II)

In *Tristram Shandy*, Sterne takes the and in dance of a peasant girl, as a lame youth plays the pipe and his sister, "who had stolen her voice from heaven," sings a "Gascoigne roundelay," "Viva la joia!".

> -Why could I not live, and end my days thus? Just Disposer of our joys and sorrows, cried I, why

could not a man sit down in the lap of content here-and dance, and sing, and say his prayers, and go to heaven with this nut-brown maid?

(Bk. VII, Ch. 43)

Similarly, in *A Sentimental Journey,* Sterne leaves the "beggarly system" of flattery amongst the "children of art" in Paris, again in pursuit of "nature," and finds it in the peasant family:

-It was a little farmhouse surrounded with about twenty acres of vineyard, full of everything which could make plenty in a French peasant's house...

The family consisted of an old grey-headed man and his wife, with five or six sons and sons-in-law, and their several wives, and a joyous genealogy out of 'em.

They were all sitting down together to their lentil-soup; a large wheaten loaf was in the middle of the table; and a flaggon of wine at each end of it promised joy through the stages of the repast - 'twas a feast of love.

The old man rose up to meet me, and with a respectful cordiality would have me sit down at the table; my heart was sat down the moment I entered the room; so I sat down at once like a son of the family...

When supper was over, the old man gave a knock upon the table with the haft of his knife - to bid them prepare for the dance...

> It was not till the middle of the second dance, when, from some pauses in the movement wherein they all seemed to look up, I fancied I could distinguish an elevation of spirit different from that which is the cause or the effect of simple jollity-In a word, I thought I beheld Religion mixing in the dance...
> (Book Two, "The Supper")

The language in both episodes of the dance tend towards mythic largeness and comprehensiveness, as the rhythms of country, of family and village life are symbolized as a ordered, traditional folk dance: life seen as music rather than discord.

◆

Life is however, harmonious only intermittently; so counsels Samuel Johnson, the moral sage of the 18th century, in everything he has written. Any secular myth that may temporarily console us cannot answer our spiritual hunger as religious hopes may do; thus Johnson's Christian existentialism. Johnson endured life-long bouts with melancholia and his moral essays are pervaded with a sadness and a sober unwillingness to give himself up to wishful thinking about life. Family, marriage, and social intercourse in general are seen as usually flawed and inadequate.

And yet Johnson can say in Rambler 68, "To be happy at home is the ultimate result of all ambition, the end to which every enterprise and labour tends..." Johnson in his old age returns briefly to the village of his youth to stand "for a considerable time bareheaded in the rain, on the spot where my father's stall used to stand", and the reason was that once in his youth, "I was disobedient; I refused to attend my father to Uttoxeter market. Pride was the source of that refusal, and the rememberance of it was painful... In contrition I stood, and I hope the penance was expiatory"! Johnson's mother was "a woman of distinguished understanding," as was Johnson's wife; his devotion to both is outlined in Boswell's *Johnson*. But at the time we meet Johnson in Boswell, Johnson has lost both mother and wife, and has made, as best he could and in spite of his chronic melancholia, a surrogate family out of those to whom he gave charity, including lodging in his apartments, and those intellectual companions in the coffee houses of London, the London which becomes the loved neighborhood of a tortured and great spirit.

Johnson in his loneliness provides an early symbol, for all of his neo-classicism, for the coming age of romanticism, which will find in Quixote a symbol of its own tragic alienation. The Nineteenth Century can be examined in terms of both the triumph and the anguish of the individual ego. The solitary self, that aloneness which Johnson feared, becomes the dominant subject of art, as the effects of industrial and scientific revolutions put terrible strains on both extended and nuclear families and on rootedness in general. The literature of the high culture of the West in the Nineteenth and Twentieth Centuries perhaps exaggerates these atomistic and anomic tendencies when it does not treat of the vigorous and still enduring folk cultures and literatures and their contexts of strong familialism and localism. But there is no question that, as Matthew Arnold has said of his century, "the dialogue of the mind with itself has commenced." ("Preface" to *Poems*, 1853).

The greatest of the poets writing in English in the modern world, Wordsworth, Yeats, Eliot, Williams, and others, will lament the loss of rootedness, of family, of the peasantry and regionalism, but the bulk of their poems will be of alienation. Wordsworth's "Preface" to the *Lyrical Ballads* (1800) is largely of the virtues of the peasantry, and the poet is at a time in his life when he has spurned the worlds of Paris and London and returned to the beloved English Lake District of his upbringing. Wordsworth, in the great period of his writing 1797-1806, is however a solitary, musing the implications of what he sees as a fading transcendental gift. The losses experienced by whatever local persons he introduces in his poems, Michael, Margaret, the lover of Lucy, the old leech gatherer, etc. tend to symbolize the feeling of loss of creative vision in himself. Finally, and tragically, Wordsworth come to see his creative gift itself as morally deficient, egoistic, alienated:

> A power is gone, which nothing can restore;
> A deep distress hath humanised my Soul...

Farewell, farewell the heart that lives alone,
Housed in a dream, at distance from the Kind!
"Elegaic Stanzas" (1805)

Coleridge, Wordsworth's collaborator in the *Lyrical Ballads*, has similar feelings of loss and alienation in "Dejection, an Ode," feelings that Arnold later in "The Scholar Gypsy" calls the "infection of our mental strife."

In the worlds of the novel, the modern intellectual malaise diagnosed by the romantic poets enters a bit later. Jane Austen's world is of an Eighteenth Century provincial society where class and family are both traditional and stable. Charles Dickens' *Pickwick Papers* (1837), a generation later, evokes a world, on the road and in the villages and the City, much like that of Smollett's *Humphry Clinker*. Mr. Pickwick himself is drawn to the lineaments of the Eighteenth Century idiosyncratic and benevolent gentleman. But later the world of *Hard Times* (1854), the hideous Coketown and the anomie of the displaced industrial worker, Stephen Blackpool, comes to dominate Dickens' creative imagination. We are given two great symbols of decline in the Victorian Age in poor Cratchit's loving and desperate attempts to hold a family together in *A Christmas Carol* (1843) and in Sir Leicester Dedlock's falling asleep "for the good of the country" in *Bleak House* (1853). The old familial and rural social order seems to be dying and any new order seems, in Arnold's phrase, "powerless to be born".

The two greatest of Russian novelists, Tolstoy and Dostoyevsky, attempt, with enormous power, to counter this alienation in the modern intellectual consciousness. Their arguments are ultimately religious, but are strongly shaped by their feelings for the Russian soil, the peasantry, and the family.

The major questing character of *War and Peace* (1865), the nobleman Pierre Buzuhov, after worshipping at the altars of many false idols, has a quasi-religious epiphany while he is imprisoned by the French and observes the Russian peasant Platon Karataev. Karataev's conversation is filled with the proverbs of a Sancho Panza, though more pertinently applied, and his values are those of family:

> 'And are your old parents living?' he asked, and though Pierre could not see him in the dark, he felt that the soldier's lips were puckered in a restrained smile of kindliness while he asked these questions. He was evidently disappointed that Pierre had no parents, especially that he had not a mother... 'And have you children?' he went on to ask. Pierre's negative reply seemed to disappoint him again, and he added himself: 'Oh well, you are young folks; please God, there will be. Only live in peace and concord...Father says all his children are alike; whichever finger's pricked, it hurts the same.' (Pt. XII, Ch. XII)

Buzuhov is permanently transformed by his experience with Karataev:

> For a long while Pierre did not sleep, and lay with open eyes in the darkness...and he felt that the world that had been shattered was rising up now in his soul, in new beauty and on new foundations that could not be shaken... Platon Karataev remained for ever in his mind the strongest and most precious memory, and the personification of everything Russian, kindly, and round.
> (Pt. XII, Ch. XII-XIII)

Pierre ultimately marries the charming Natasha Rostov, and their marriage quickly moves to what Tolstoy clearly feels is a deeper dimension than the "romantic":

> She felt that the tie that bound her to her husband did not rest on those romantic feelings which had attracted him to her, but rested on something else undefined, but as strong as the tie that bound her soul to her body...
>
> The subject in which Natasha was completely absorbed was her family, that is, her husband, whom she kept such a hold on so that he should belong entirely to her, to his home and her children, whom she had to carry, to bear, to nurse and to bring up.
>
> And the more she put, not her mind only, but her whole soul, her whole being, into the subject that absorbed her, the more that subject seemed to enlarge under her eyes, and the feebler and the

more inadequate her own powers seemed for coping with it. ("Epilogue," Pt. I, Ch. X)

The tragic heroine of *Anna Karenina* (1875) could not cope with her marriage and family; her romantic feelings were for another lover; it is as the famous first sentence of the novel states, "Happy families are all alike; every unhappy family is unhappy in its own way."

Konstantin Levin, the aristocratic landowner, in *Karenina,* speaks for the moral struggle and search of Count Leo Tolstoy, the novel's creator:

If he had been asked whether he liked or didn't like the peasants, Konstantin Levin would have been absolutely at a loss what to reply. He liked and did not like the peasants, just as he liked and did not like men in general. Of course, being a good-hearted man, he liked men rather than he disliked them, and so too with the peasants. But like or dislike "the people" as something apart he could not, not only because he lived with "the people," and all his interests were bound up with theirs, but also because he regarded himself as a part of "the people," did not see any special qualities or failings distinguishing himself and "the people," and could not contrast himself with them.

(Trans. C. Garnett. Random House, 1939, Pt. III, Ch. I)

The peasants on Levin's estate might have much to teach him. In a scene reminiscent of Sterne's invitations to the dance with the French peasants in *Tristram Shandy* and *A Sentimental Journey*, Levin observes a peasant dance with pangs of separation:

> the whole meadow and distant fields all seemed to be shaking and singing to the measures of this wild merry song with its shouts and whistles and clapping. Levin felt envious of this health and mirthfulness; he longed to take part in the expression of this joy of life. But he could do nothing, and had to lie and look on and listen. When the peasants, with their singing, had vanished out of sight and hearing, a weary feeling of despondency at his own isolation, his physical inactivity, his alienation from this world, came over Levin. (Pt. III, Ch. XII)

However much he admires the life of "simplicity and toil," he knows that he "cannot go back to it."

He marries the aristocratic Kitty Shtcherbatsky, happily in the main, but still driven to search for a personal yet universal faith

> to complete that great miracle, continually manifest upon earth, that made it possible for each man and millions of different sorts of men, wise men and imbeciles, old men and children-all men, peasants, Lvov, Kitty, beggars and kings to

understand perfectly the same one thing, and to build up thereby that life of the soul which alone is worth living, and which alone is precious to us.
(Pt. VIII, Ch. XIII)

It is a faith that the young Alyosha Karamazov in Dostoyevsky's *The Brother Karamazov* (1880) seems to have instinctively, and yet surprisingly, given the history of his family. He has been brought up in various homes after the death of his pious mother at the age of four, his father, a disgusting reprobate, having all but abandoned him. His one brother, Dimitri, is an impulsive sensualist, and another, Ivan, a tortured intellectual heretic. Alyosha's personality may however have been early defined by the faintest memory of his mother praying at home before an icon of the Virgin, as he intimates to a group of young boys at the end of the novel:

> You must know that there is nothing higher and stronger and more wholesome and good for life in the future than some good memory, especially a memory of childhood, of home. People talk to you a great deal about your education, but some good, sacred memory, preserved from childhood, is perhaps the best education. If a man carries many such memories with him into life, he is safe to the end of his days. (Trans. C. Garnett, The Modern Library, 1943, "Epilogue," Ch. 3)

Aloysha strives throughout the novel to keep the love between the three brothers intact, aided by the counsel of his spiritual father, the holy monk, Father Zossima. But Dimitri, for all of his benevolence, cannot control his impulses, and Ivan, for all of his desire for a faith which could give a foundation for the values he wants to hold, cannot believe. In a fit of brain fever, Ivan hallucinates a devil, with whom he speaks:

> What I dream of is becoming incarnate once for all and irrevocably in the form of some merchant's wife weighing eighteen stone, and of believing all she believes. My ideal is to go to church and offer a candle in simple-hearted faith, upon my word it is. Then there would be an end to my sufferings.
> (Book XI, Ch. IX)

The young Tonio Kröger in Thomas Mann's novella (1903) similarly yearns for the "bourgeois" and the "commonplace," as he watches Ingeborg Holm dancing from behind french doors. She does not love him, and Tonio goes off to Southern Europe and becomes a famous writer. Eventually however, at the end of the novella, he will write to an artistic confidante:

> "I stand between two worlds. I am at home in neither, and I suffer in consequence. You artists call me a bourgeois, and the bourgeois try to arrest

me...you ought to realize that there is a way of being an artist that goes so deep and is so much a matter of origins and destinies that no longing seems to it sweeter and more worth knowing than longing after the bliss of the commonplace.

"I admire those proud, cold beings who adventure upon the paths of great and daemonic beauty and despise 'mankind'; but I do not envy them. For if anything is capable of making a poet of a literary man, it is my bourgeois love of the human, the living and usual. It is the source of all warmth, goodness, and humour.

(Trans H. T. Lowe-Porter, N.Y. Vintage Books, 1954, p. 133).

As religious faith was undermined during the Nineteenth Century, a worship of art had seemed for a while to be a possible home for the spirit, but by the opening decades of the Twentieth Century, the artist seemed sorely tried to hold to values beyond or even including the "commonplace," the "human, the living and usual."

The culmination of a modern sense of irony towards the Western Judeo-Christian and Hellenic values, mythologies, and idealisms, is in James Joyce's *Ulysses* (1923), whose very title stresses its ironic counterpointing to Homer's sense of values. Joyce's modern day Ulysses, Leopold Bloom, is a "disinherited Jew" whose country, Ireland, does not really accept him. He has left the faith of his fathers though he has retained fond memories of his father and mother; he mourns his lost son Rudy, dotes on his young daughter Milly, and for all of his pathetic philandering during this period of what is really his wife Molly's first excursion into adultery, is as much in love, in his fashion, with her as she is with him, in her fashion. Stephen Daedalus, the young Irish artist, has torn himself (with great guilt) from family, religion and country, and seeks a spiritual home, father, and family in the realm of art. Three thousand years of Western cultural heritage are rendered essentially pointless through constant mock epic counterpointing to contingent Dublin everyday reality, demythologizing everything in that heritage in the process. And yet for all this devaluation, there is a sense of irreducible humanity of family feeling, in Bloom and in Molly, which triumphs in the book.

Bloom's thoughts as he observes Simon Daedalus, Stephen's father:

> Noisy selfwilled man. Full of his son. He is right. Something to hand on. If little Rudy had lived. See him grow up. Hear his voice in the house. Walking beside Molly in an Eton suit. My son. Me in his eyes. Strange feeling it would be. From me. (From "Hades," *Ulysses*, Pt. II, Ch. 3)

Molly's on her husband's acquaintances:

> theyre a nice lot all of them well theyre not going

to get my husband again into their clutches if I can help it making fun of him then behind his back I know well when he goes on with his idiotics because he has sense enough not to squander every penny piece he earns down their gullets and looks after his wife and family

("Penelope," Pt. III, Ch. 3)

Without gods or heros or a viable mythology in which to believe, Joyce attempts then in *Ulysses* a most difficult feat, to sacramentalize, poeticize, the urban, the commonplace, and mundane, to make--in Hart Crane's words-- "a grail of laughter of an empty ash can" ("Chaplinesque"), Dublin without the Naiads of Homer's Ithaca. Joyce succeeds so far as his self-irony will allow him.

Hart Crane himself has argued in *The Bridge* the sophisticated modern position, that mythologies of place and presences sustain man and societies, and that myth-making will, must, go on even in an age of unbelief. It is a position which is central to the attitudes of a good number of major Twentieth Century poets (as I have outlined in previous books of mine).

Wallace Stevens, in language that used to be reserved for prayers to gods and goddesses, sings to "the One of Fictive Music," that is, to his own creative imagination (elsewhere, his "interior paramour"), which fashions temporary paradises of our surroundings:

> Now, of the music summoned by the birth
> That separates us from the wind and sea,
> Yet leaves us in them, until earth becomes,
> By being so much of the things we are,
> Gross effigy and simulacrum, none
> Gives motion to perfection more serene
> Than yours, out of our imperfections wrought...
>
> For so retentive of themselves are men
> That music is intensest which proclaims
> The near, the clear, and vaunts the clearest bloom

Man will make music and it will be music of the "near," of one's own "local objects," as the poet in "Bantams in Pine Woods" "points" the "Appalachian tangs" of his locale, not the pines of any and all locales.

Robert Frost in symbolizing his creative imagination uses imagery of a New England brook or stream. In Frost's view, the modern poet like himself must try to decide "what to make of a diminished thing" ("Oven Bird"): his brook is not Castalia, the rushing stream of Greek pastorale, but a thin brook close to the village house:

> A brook to none but who remember long.
> This as it will be seen is other far
> Than with brooks taken otherwhere in song.
> We love the things we love for what they are.
> 				("Hyla Brook")

A child's treehouse imaginings figure both the past's mythologies and those of modern poets':

> The height of the adventure is the height
> Of country where two village cultures faded
> Into each other. Both of them are lost.
>   ...The only field
> Now left's no bigger than a harness gall...
> Your destination and your destiny's
> A brook that was the water of the house...
> I have kept hidden in the instep arch
> Of an old cedar at the waterside
> A broken drinking goblet like the Grail
> Under a spell so the wrong ones can't find it...
> Here are your waters and your watering place.
> Drink and be whole again beyond confusion.
>   ("Directive")

The mind is the "only field" where the memories of lost village cultures remain, there where the stream of feelings issue from the imagination into art. The localism and sacramentalism that used to pervade earlier societies is still preserved, says Frost, in the surviving village cultures and in the creative imagination.

 Yeats collected the folklore of the Irish peasantry and in "Under Ben Bulben" asked the Irish poets who would come after him to "sing the peasantry."

> John Synge, I and Augusta Gregory, thought
> All that we did, all that we said or sang
> Must come from contact with the soil, from that
> Contact everything Antaeus-like grew strong.
> ("The Municipal Gallery Revisited")

Of Lady Gregory's estate, Coole Park, and Lady Gregory herself, Yeats has written these lines of archetypal localism and familialism:

> Great rooms where travelled men and children found
> Content or joy; a last inheritor
> Where none has reigned that lacked a name and fame...
>
> A spot whereon the founders lived and died
> Seemed once more dear than life; ancestral trees,
> Or gardens rich in memory glorified
> Marriages, alliances and families,
> And every bride's ambition satisfied...
> We were the last romantics-chose for theme
> Traditional sanctity and loveliness;
> Whatever's written in what poets name
> The book of the people; whatever most can bless
> The mind of man or elevate a rhyme
> ("Coole Park and Ballylee, 1931")

And for his daughter Yeats prayed for similar archetypes:

> May she become a flourishing hidden tree...
> O may she live like some green laurel
> Rooted in one dear perpetual place...
> And may her bridegroom bring her to a house
> Where all's accustomed, ceremonious;
> Ceremony's a name for the rich horn,
> And custom for the spreading laurel tree.
>
> (" A Prayer for My Daughter")

The imagery of the early poetry of T.S. Eliot is largely of disintegration in Western culture, though here and there in *The Wasteland* and elsewhere one finds strains of an earlier music of social harmony, of Spenser's *Epithalamion*, or of the folk in tune with deep rhythms of life:

> O City city, I can sometimes hear
> Beside a public bar in Lower Thames Street,
> The pleasant whining of a mandoline
> And a clatter and a chatter from within
> Where fishmen lounge at noon...
>
> (III, "The Fire Sermon")

Eliot then in his later prose:

> But by far the most important channel of transmission of culture remains the family: and when family life fails to play its part, we must expect our culture to deteriorate... But when I speak of the family, I have in mind a bond which

embraces a longer period of time than this: a piety towards the dead, however obscure, and a solicitude for the unborn, however remote...It is important that a man should feel himself to be, not merely a citizen of a particular nation, but a citizen of a particular part of his country, with local loyalties. These... arise out of loyalty to the family...
    (*Notes Towards the Definition of Culture*, Ch's II & III)

Which are pretty much the propositions I have tried to present in this essay.

    As I intimated earlier (above p 57), Ezra Pound, Eliot's friend and peer, loved local rituals of veneration, sanctification of place (though he had "no dogma"), and the Confucian ideal of familial loyalty. In his "Pisan Cantos" Pound invokes "Taishan-Chocorua" as he looks out over the Pisan hills. That is, no matter what sacred mountain one invokes, one from the Orient, or New England, or Tuscany, every high place needs a temple, every grove needs an altar, where man can venerate one's gods, family and region. And, like another friend, Joyce, Pound uses throughout his *Cantos* Homer's *Odyssey* as a paradigm for Western Civilization at its most humane.

    William Carlos Williams is less sanguine than Eliot or Pound about the possibility of retaining the past in the present. He expressed his delight at the folk dance in Breughel's "The Kermiss," but says in his "Raleigh Was Right" that "We cannot go to the country," for the time "when country people/ Would plough and sow with/ Flowering minds" is gone, and now, "Love itself is a flower/ With roots in a parched ground," the Twentieth Century. Our America, Williams asserts in "The Pure Products of America," suffers from "imaginations which have no/ peasant traditions to give them/ character." Our pastorale, he says, must be of urban music, as Williams has learned to appreciate it:

> I walk back streets
> admiring houses
> of the very poor:
> roof out of line with sides,
> the yards cluttered
> with old chicken wire, ashes,
> furniture gone wrong...   ("Pastorale")
>
> It's the anarchy of poverty
> delights me, the old
> yellow wooden house indented
> among the new brick tenements
>
> Chimneys, roofs, fences of
> wood and metal in an unfenced
> age and enclosing next to
> nothing at all: the old man
> in a sweater and soft black
> hat who sweeps the sidewalk...   ("The Poor")

Williams is doctor to the poor and deeply sympathetic to them, but his final diagnosis is of a spiritual sickness pervading our times which makes him prefer the decaying neighborhoods with social personality to the "new brick tenements" of anonymity.

I walk my neighborhood surrounded by the presences of those immigrants, friends, relatives and family, many long gone, who gave these streets and homes vitality for me. I remember my mother and father talking to fruit trees, vegetables and animals as if they were understanding them. They had no doubt that the blessed Wind was a direct and miraculous gift from God, Who most likely spoke Lebanese rather than Italian, or whatever. And as I walk and remember, I am with those, like Robert Nesbit and Michael Novak, who believe that familialism and localism are among the values "most durable in the history of civilization," that the family is the "absolutely critical center of social force" and the "primary teacher of moral development."

Ivan Karamazov's corrosive intellect was balanced by his hunger for an immortality which might justify life's tragedies. Miguel de Unamuno, in his *The Tragic Sense of Life*, argues that Ivan's hunger is ineradicable in the human spirit and that therefore, even in the absence of rational belief, we must live so as to deserve immortality. I find this will to believe (the term of course is William James') a good formula for a life, because it precludes nothing. It allows me to bless imaginative life in all of its variousness, past and present, the song and story of both poet and peasant, myth rooted in the here and now, the commonplace, the familial and the local, yearning, to be sure, towards the universal and the true, but achieving, at least, the beautiful. It is with me, perhaps, as it is with Konstantin Levin in *Anna Karenina*:

> Lying on his back, he gazed up now into the high, cloudless sky. "Do I not know that that is infinite space, and that it is not a round arch? But, however I screw up my eyes and strain my sight, I cannot see it not round and not bounded, and in spite of my knowing about infinite space, I am incontestably right when I see a solid blue dome, and more right than when I strain my eyes to see beyond it."
> Levin ceased thinking, and only, as it were, listened to mysterious voices that seemed talking joyfully and earnestly within him.
> (Pt. VIII, Ch. XIII)

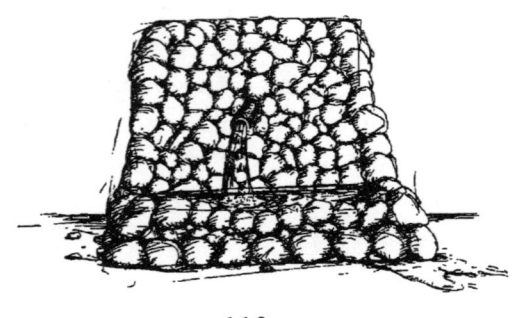

Chapter Three

Family and Village in Folk Literature: Some Lebanese and Sicilian Examples

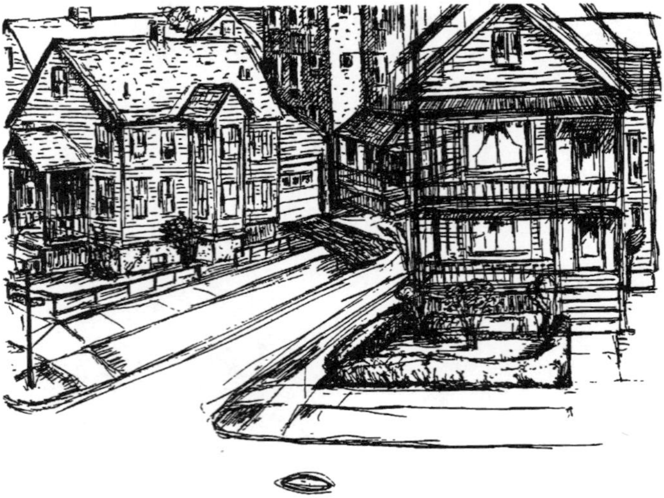

It was my late (and deeply missed) brother, thirteen years my senior, who introduced me to great works of Western Literature, feeding me, from the age of twelve, books "that I might be interested in," guiding without pressuring, as the best teachers do. It was my brother in fact who took me by the hand at the age of four down the block to the local library and taught me to read. *Ferdinand the Bull* was my first book and thereafter I walked down that block to the library once a week till I left the neighborhood for college.

That ethnic neighborhood of Italian and Lebanese immigrants was a wonderful place to grow up, and it was a most happy childhood. My father was a mill worker, eventually a foreman in a plaster mill, very hard work with few rewards. I was younger than my two brothers by nine and thirteen years; I looked up to them, and as often as I could I followed them around after school. And when my father finally came home from work, I would follow him around. It often seemed to me that I was not really separate from my father and brothers, but a part of them. In the evening, if my father and my mother, whom I worshipped, did not visit the homes of other Lebanese, or have visitors to us, I would walk with my father to the Arabic coffee house or *Ah'we*, to watch the men play pinochle and to wait for the many treats they would give me. This constant round of visiting, of having visitors, the immigrant streets full of people, the constant sidewalk, stoop and porch conversations, and the many hours at the kitchen table listening to stories, to the vivid imaginations of my parents and those of their generation, to their values and their humor, all of this flowed into my spirit as the spring flow into the branch or vine. I never felt that I was only a little child meant to play with other little children, although that was all right too. I was first of all a part of a family, part of my father and of my mother and brothers, and part of a vital neighborhood.

Certainly this ethnic, peasant, Mediterranean upbringing affected my reading predilections as a child, as an adolescent, and as an adult. I know now why, try as hard as I could (for I did feel guilty), I could not maintain much of a reading interest in what I was told by my teachers I *should* love, Grimms' and other fairy tales, tales of mythological heros and monsters, of the more fantastical of the *Arabian Nights*, or other tales of implausible adventure. These were of extremes of experience or imagination, whether of brutality or fear, or of marvel or miracle. I much preferred, at home, the humorous stories of my parents' generation concerning the village fool, or lazy man, or corrupt official, or the beautiful girl next door, or, at the library, Robert McCloskey's Lentil playing his harmonica or William Saroyan's Aram on the beautiful white horse.

I know now that one finally looks in literature for the values one wants to affirm, in my case the cultural values of my parents, and that these are metacritical predilections that one can share only partially with another reader who has come from a different cultural context of values. And yet, having said this, it seems to me there is far more to share in central human values than to separate, as I hope these essays demonstrate.

The eminent sociologist Herbert Gans, in an introduction to Jerre Mangione's classic "memoir of Italian American life" *Mount Allegro* (an italian immigrant neighborhood of Rochester N.Y.), could have just as well been speaking of my neighborhood (including its Lebanese population) of East Utica:

> The mainstay of Mount Allegro social life and the heart of the book are the "stories" that family members told each other during their nearly nightly gatherings. Some are dramatic renderings of neighborhood gossip; others are similar gossip from the old country now transformed into folk tales. A handful are or were once true; many have always been apocryphal. Some are tragic, most are funny, but virtually all are morality playlets which uphold and defend the immigrants' major values against real or imagined subverters...Indeed, one of Mangione's enduring contributions is his committing the oral tradition to paper, thus

preserving the stories for folklorists, students of ethics and morality, and of course social scientists and historians.

I would add "students of literature" as well, for in the hands of a Mangione, or an Italo Calvino, or a Cervantes or a Chaucer, or even the gifted immigrant storyteller or poet down the block, the folktale or song can reach the level of high art.

I have written my own memoir of growing up Lebanese-American in East Utica. It is called *Wind of the Land* (the title is itself taken from Lebanese folksong) and the book is in large measure defined by the values and the stories and songs of my parents and their generation, immigrants from the Christian Mt. Lebanon before W.W.I. I would like a bit later to offer translations of mine of some of these stories and songs that I have on tape either in my mother's Arabic or that of one of her peers, together with commentary, literary and sociological, on the pieces themselves and on the immigrant values of family and place that are at their core. First, I would like to take a brief look at the intellectual tradition I found in place when as a young student of English Literature I instinctively sought to justify my own predilections for such folk literature.

I have spoken earlier of Jonathan Swift's own social values, of his respect for the "common forms" of humanity, as symbolized in the ordered estate of Lord Munodi in Pt. 3 Ch. 4 of *Gulliver's Travels*.

(above p. 82) Concomitant with this idea of common central values is Swift's continual satiric attack on the extremes of literary "fancy" and of religious "enthusiasm," using as images of such extremes running references to fairy, heroic, and mythological tales:

> The first Piece I have handled is that of *Tom Thumb*, whose Author was a *Pythagorean* Philosopher. This dark Treatise contains the whole Scheme of the *Metempsychosis*, deducing the Progress of the Soul thro' all her Stages...I shall not trouble you with recounting what Adventures they met for the first seven Years, any farther than by taking notice, that they carefully observed their Father's Will...That they travelled thro' several Countries, encountred a reasonable Quantity of Gyants and slew certain Dragons...But Heroick Virtue it self hath not been exempt from the Obloquy of Evil Tongues. For it hath been objected, that those Antient Heroes, famous for their Combating so many Giants, and Dragons, and Robbers, were in their own Persons a greater Nuisance to Mankind, than any of those Monsters they subdued; and therefore, to render their Obligations more Compleat, when all *other* Vermin were destroy'd, should in Conscience have concluded with the same Justice upon themselves: as *Hercules* most generously did, and hath upon that Score, procured to himself more

Temples and Votaries than the best of his Fellows.
Tale of a Tub Sec's I, II, & III.

Sam Johnson's equal antipathy to fairy, myth, and the incredible is more discursively argued in many places in his critical writings:

> To select a singular event, and swell it to a giant's bulk by fabulous appendages of spectres and predictions, has little difficultly, for he that forsakes the probable may always find the marvellous. (life of *Grey*)

> Other dramatists can only gain attention by hyperbolical or aggravated characters, by fabulous and unexampled excellence or depravity, as the writers of barbarous romances invigorated the reader by a giant and a dwarf; and he that should form his expectations of human affairs from the play, or from the tale, would be equally deceived. *Shakespeare* has no heroes: his scenes are occupied only by men. (Preface to *Shakespeare*)

Johnson disliked the "fictions" of the "Fancy" or what he called the "Imagination" because its "inventions" would ignore the plausible and probable in life, where gods and heros in machines do not conquer evil, where the bad do not often get better, and where the good are prone to false expectation. Johnson's aim for art then was to avoid setting up false abstractions or symbols, to look so long and hard at life that the general truths of a common humanity would emerge. This puts forward the ideal of commonality, universality, centrality, normality, in the nature of mankind which captivated Swift and many others in the 18th century and after, and which captivates me. It is an ideal which cannot be proven, but which can be captivating enough (and true enough) to give a focus to one's life and values. To restate the position using Johnson's metaphor in *Rassalas*, the artist must look long and hard at hundreds of individual tulips, not for the eccentricities, but to sense in them the archetypal tulip of perfect parts, a tulip which might never exist in nature, but which is close enough to possibility to lift one's spirit in that direction.

> ...authors are at liberty, tho' not to invent, yet to select objects, and to cull from the mass of mankind, those individuals upon which the attention ought most to be employ'd; as a diamond, though it cannot be made, may be polished by art...
>
> It is justly considered as the greatest excellency of art, to imitate nature; but it is necessary to distinguish those parts of nature, which are most proper for imitation: greater care is still required in representing life, which is so often discoloured by passion, or deformed by wickedness. If the world be promiscuously described, I cannot see of what use it can be to read the account. *Rambler* #4

The preceding encompasses a body of ideas with I have a great deal of sympathy. The focus of the artist and reader is turned away from the singular, the extreme, to the common and to the center, what Thomas Mann calls in *Tonio Kroger* the "bliss of the commonplace," the "love of the human, the living and usual," the "source of all warmth, goodness, and humor" (see above, p. 99).

In his *The Science of Folklore* (1930), Alexander Krappe offers a clear definition of one sort of folk literature depicting "ordinary human life," which I am here stressing and distinguishes it from the fairy tale:

> By *merry tale* we mean a short narrative, in prose or verse, relating an episodical event or series of events culminating in a humorous situation. Its subject-matter is taken from everyday life: the occurrence of supernatural elements is rare and even then serves only to create the basis underlying the situation, not the situation itself...In so far as the merry tale depicts ordinary human life and presupposes the most elementary relationships such as kinship and kinship by marriage, those of master and servant, priest and layman, etc., its territory is not nearly so circumscribed as is that of the fairy tale...The merry tale, in other words, is not bound to any definite society but floats freely from country to country.
>
> Under these circumstances it must be admitted that the merry tale is properly speaking ageless in

the sense that it must have sprung up the moment man formed a certain social organization, however rudimentary...collections of merry tales have existed from the dawn of ancient civilization. Evidently they have by their very nature a wider appeal than fairy stories. (Chap. II)

I have been reading in the scholarly literature on folktale and song in Stith Thompson, Richard Dorson, Italo Calvino, and others, so as to introduce myself to the systematic study of the issues in the discipline. What I propose now to do is to offer some examples from the folk literature I know best from my own Lebanese-American cultural heritage, examining these pieces both from the viewpoints these essays of mine have been developing and some of the issues that are developed in the discipline.

There was in the Wadi El Arayesh in the Lebanese Mountains a young man dopey, clumsy, slow, baggy-trousered, hair over his eyes, and too stupid to know when to wipe his nose. And his family did not know what to do with him, as they had him sitting always outside the house with the birds perching on his head. One day then Habeeb, a member of the family, traveled to the ancient hill town of Furzol, a short way down the road from the Wadi. He visited there a friend he had not seen for years, and while taking coffee and almonds beneath the grapevine he noticed at the back of the house sitting with the chickens a young lady, certainly three hundred pounds, obese, inert, the chickens running around her legs.

"Ya Antoon, my heart's blood, is that your lovely daughter?"

"Yes, the devil take her, a pig resembling her mother's uncles."

"But a beautiful face, and loved by the animals like a saint. Is she not yet married?"

"Married! No, no, not married, though we have had dozens of suitors. We are naturally saving her for someone special."

"Antoon, my brother, we must think of family. Would you consider my sister Badoura's son, certainly unworthy for your daughter, but clever in his own way."

"To bring our families together, young man of my heart, anything, and there is no other family to which I would say this. Without seeing the young man, my daughter is yours."

And so a wedding was arranged on the spot for two days hence. Back to the Wadi ran Habeeb to his sister Badoura and then to his brothers and they all exulted in this good fortune that had come to the family. And they wiped the young man's nose and washed and dressed him on the wedding morning and they all marched out of the village on the road to Furzol, singing and shooting their guns in celebration. Till half way there and with backward glances at their nephew, who was staring at his feet as he walked, the men of the Wadi grew fearful.

"Ya Habeeb, the men of Furzol will never accept this jackass when they see him. Our walk will be for nothing."

"You have read my thoughts, brother Juryus, and the Lord perhaps has just blessed me with the answer. Let us leave our dear nephew hidden here by the hillside with the women. And we will go on and tell the men of Furzol that the groom has taken ill. But that we are so eager to join families that we wish to lead their beauteous daughter to our village to marry our beloved nephew at his bedside in a small ceremony with little fuss."

Again they shot their guns and sang, and the three brothers marched with happy mind and alone to Furzol.

Approaching the village and as yet unseen, the brothers heard laughter and shouting from the houses of Antoon and his brothers. And they paused to listen, hiding behind the wall of the first house in the village.

"Ya men of Furzol and of the House of Slymann, Father of Antoon, today we will have put one over again on the blind buffoons, those dumb peasants of Wadi El Arayesh!"

To which Habeeb winked his eye to his brothers behind the wall and said:

"Wait, O Bears of Furzol, till you find what's waiting for you down the road a little way by the hillside!"

One has loyalty in Mount Lebanon first of all to family, albeit a very widely extended family, and its friends, then to one's religious sect, and then to one's village, hardly at all to one's region or nation-state. The men of Wadi El Arayesh mock and attempt to swindle those of Furzol, and vice-versa, but the men of both villages realize that the creation of new family ties between solid, freeholding families is mutually advantageous. Neither Habeeb nor Antoon is fooled by the other's polite and hyperbolic Arabic in arranging the marriage between the families, but the diction is seen as a civilized and civilizing convention. Neither family is really gaining an advantage over the other, and even if it transpired that one family did, there would be other days, in what seemed, at least till our time, to be an endless history in a continuous social culture. The men of Furzol are called by Habeeb "dibs," which means "wild bears," which means uncivilized. But it isn't so. We are dealing here with ancient, highly sophisticated folk culture as expressed in stories in a highly ornate and intricate Arabic. Much of the joy in the stories for the listeners is in their catching ironies and cues in the changing level in the diction and its decorums, giving them a sense of belonging, of mastery of a given social continuum or order.

And then, one must say, there is an added dimension to the tale as it is told over and again in America by the first generation immigrants: a sense of sweet pain as the emigre recalls the hill village of his youth and the joy of belonging there, as he faces what seemed to him the slow obliteration of one's values and one's family life in America. This added tragic dimension of cherished things passing away is one that can lift folk tale to the level of high art.

The story is a fairly literal translation of mine of one of my late mother's Arabic folktales and songs recollected from her youth on a tape recording I urged her to make shortly before her death. She had had no opportunity for eduction in Lebanon and could read no Arabic (although she was very bright and had taught herself to read and write English). She was herself brought up in the Wadi El Arayesh, and I should add that one of my bright and beautiful cousins from the Wadi is now married to a good man from Furzol. Also that on my way to Lebanon to visit my relatives for the first and only time in 1960, I traveled with an East Utica Italian-American friend of mine and we stopped first in *his* ancestral hill village of Amato, Catanzaro, in Southern Italy. We met his aged grandfather, who still chuckled over the fact that his son had gone to American and married there a girl from Castagna, that "ridiculous" village ten miles down the road and on the next mountaintop. Furzol or Castagna, the attitude is much the same and has always been on the Mediterranean, if not simply in the human heart. Witness the Florentine lady Pampinea's attitude towards Venice as she begins the second tale of the fourth day in Boccaccio's *Decameron*:

there was once in Imola a man of wicked and corrupt ways named Berto della Massa, whose evil deeds were so well known by the people of Imola that nobody there would believe him when he told the truth, not to mention when he lied. Realizing that his tricks would no longer work there, in desperation he moved to Venice, that receptacle of all forms of wickedness...Now it happened that there was a foolish and silly young woman named Madonna Lisetta da Ca'Quirino...a Venetian (and, as such, a gossip like all of them)...

I had a young friend from Lebanon hear my mother's tape recently and he asserted that he had heard this tale back in his village, that he was told by his grandmother that the tale was based on a true incident, but it was told of the villages of Furzol and Ablah, not Furzol and the Wadi. The Ablah family was of course not the Wadi family my mother had mentioned. My mother had also told me that the tale was based on an actual occurrence. I told myself then that while it was likely that a true incident in Lebanon was the origin of the tale and that Furzol was probably originally involved, I would bet that Ablah was a less likely second village than the Wadi, since it was a much longer walk from Furzol. My bet was also that the young man's family enjoyed making Ablah the second village because of some personal satiric purpose.

These are still likely suppositions even after

looking up the motifs in this tale in the standard indexes to Folk-Literature. One does not in fact find a similar tale with similar motifs either in the *Types of the Folk-Tale* of Aarne-Thompson (1928) or the six volume *Motif-Index of Folk Literature* of Thompson (1964). This might be construed as evidence of the unique origin of the folktale in Lebanon at a certain historical moment, when there occurred a certain arranged marriage between two actual dumbbells. And yet I must report that in recently rereading *Don Quixote* after thirty years, I did find a brilliant analog to my Lebanese tale in the petitions of the farmer from Miguelturra to Governor Sancho:

> this son of mine who is studying to be a bachelor has fallen in love with a lass in the same town by the name of Clara Perlerina, daughter of Andres Perlerino, another farmer and a very rich one. That name, I may tell you, is not one that has been handed down for generations but is due to the fact that all the members of this family are paralytics, ...I can only assure you, sir, that if I could but paint for you her tall figure and her bodily charms, you would find cause for astonishment; but this cannot be, for the reason that she is so bent and stooped that her knees touch her mouth, yet it is plain to be seen that if she could draw herself erect her head would scrape the roof... We are not badly matched in the matter of worldly fortune or gifts of nature; for, to

tell you the truth, Sir Governor, my son is bewitched, and there is not a day that the evil spirits do not torment him three or four times. Once he fell into the fire, and as a result his face is shriveled as a bit of parchment. His eyes, too, are somewhat watery. But he has the disposition of an angel, and if it wasn't for his always flaying and punching himself with his fist, he'd be a saint.

A few comments from the point of view of an amateur lover of some sorts of folklore. I wonder, first, why Cervantes' embellished folk tales (cf. above, p. 76) are in general not included in the *Types* or *Motif-Index* volumes (nor Boccaccio's, nor Chaucer's). Second, now knowing the Cervantes tale and of the centuries-long influence of the Arab civilization in Spain, I wonder if the motif of foolish fiancees does not go back into dim time in these cultures (as well as others), a traditional motif which then has been refashioned by both brilliant and less-than-brilliant storytellers over wide time and space. This is, of course, the usual finding of students of folk literature motifs. Finally, however, I would note that the Lebanese tale is, at least in my mother's version, richly told and sufficiently different from the Cervantes' version to stand alone as a literary work. And it is as much *of* Lebanon (the eating of almonds under the grapevine, the shooting of guns in celebration are typically Lebanese) as the Cervantes version is *of* Spain.

My mother was a born storyteller (as I am not), and it was with her (her values, her moral and artistic imagination) as it was with Italo Calvino's favorite storyteller, Agatuzza Messia of Palermo. Calvino knows her through the work of the illustrious folk scholar or ethnologist, Giuseppe Pitre:

> The secret of Pitre's work is that it gets us away from the abstract notion of "people" talking: instead, we come into contact with narrators having distinct personalities, who are identified by name, age, occupation. This makes it possible to uncover through the strata of timeless and faceless stories and through crude stereotyped expressions, traces of a personal world of more sensitive imagination, whose inner rhythm, passion, and hope are expressed through the tone of the narrator...This is how Pitre, in the preface to his anthology, describes his model narrator:
>> she has an appealing way of speaking, which makes one aware of her extraordinary memory and talent. Messia is in her seventies, is a mother, grandmother, and great-grandmother; as a little girl she heard stories from her grandmother, whose own mother had told them, having herself heard countless stories from one of her grandfathers. She had a good memory so never forgot them. There are women who hear hundreds of stories and never remember one; there are others who

remember them but haven't the knack of storytelling. Her friends in Borgo thought her a born storyteller; the more she talked, the more they wanted to listen.

(Italian Folktales, 1980, xxii - xxiii)

I remember vividly several woman of my mother's generation (as well several men) who had the "knack of storytelling" and nothing ever pleased me more than to see one or more of them pass through our kitchen door. What I present next to the reader is another story of my mother's, a story whose historical actuality I am absolutely sure about (since it happened comparatively recently in our extended family), while it yet has many of the classic ingredients of folktale.

Of the sorrowful story of Kaukeb, the beauteous daughter of Michael Asmar, and Mirhidge, son of Mirhidge Mirhidge. Who were betrothed at eleven, the priest blessing the union of families, and the fathers of each putting five gold coins in a tin box as pledge. They waited three years till Kaukeb became a woman, and she grew to love Mirhidge indeed. As for Mirhidge, no man was happier than he, when he could look out of his window and see his beloved among the fig trees, she more beautiful than the rose, large bosomed, and quick of mind and body.

But, alas, one sad day old Mirhidge was up at four and waited till seven in the fields for his son.

Returning and finding the young man sleeping, he swung his stick and berated his son as a disgrace to his family, unfit for manhood, of so worthy a woman as Kaukeb or the discriminating family of Asmar. An old deaf woman sitting among the figs heard the shouting, and imagining insults to the House of Asmar and pride in the House of Mirhidge, ran to Michael in his field. The House of Asmar would of course not brook the insult, and with Kaukeb's fierce agreement, they went into Zahle and married her on the spot to Najeeb Nackley, who had been singing her praises for years.

They shot the guns in celebration, and down came Mirhidge Mirhidge with his worthy son and all the House of Mirhidge.

"You have broken your agreement, Michael Asmar. Why have you committed so base an action, when, heretofore, no one could say a word against your family?"

"We are not used to being insulted by the Mirhidge," replied Asmar fittingly.

All was understood, and there was nothing to be done but the crying. Yet Kaukeb had a very good husband anyway and did her duty. And surely then one year later the young Mirhidge came to Michael and swore that he must have his next daughter, Annisee, and if she would not have him, he must have Fawza, the next, and if not her, he would take the baby girl in his wife's arms, and have his mother bring her up. But Annisee had always liked him. And so Michael got his five gold pieces back, which was also fitting.

Once again, family is more important than a single love or marriage tie. It is sad that Kaukeb did not have her first choice in a husband, but she herself agrees that there is no real life without family honor, so that family loyalty must take precedence over personal pleasure. There is an old saying among the Lebanese concerning the relative strengths of family versus marriage ties: "I love my bracelet, but not like my arm." I saw strength of family feeling in women, such as Kaukeb displays, as a routine matter in growing up as a Lebanese-American. I can tell you that Kaukeb's story is a true story, that of my aunt recently deceased in Lebanon who had reigned as undisputed monarch of a large clan. In fact, from all that I have seen and heard, it would seem to me that a case could be made, despite appearances, for Lebanese Christian society as to some significant degree matriarchical, insofar as decisions of real importance are quite often made by the dominant woman of a family clan. The trip to pay homage and to take counsel from the "grandmother" is a trip that one takes often in Mount Lebanon. (One such trip is beautifully described at the end of Vance Bourjaily's *Confessions of a Spent Youth*). My mother used to say, "Watch out for the woman who wants to talk about love all the time; she will be a faker!" by which my mother meant that the woman would put self before family loyalty.

The tale revolves around a misunderstanding in the mind of an old deaf woman. There is deafness in our clan and I in fact met in Lebanon the daughter of the deaf woman who precipitated this crisis of family honor. However unique the details of this story may seem, no less an authority than Antti Aarne himself has written a monograph on the pervasive motif of the deaf person precipitating a misunderstanding in folk literature. Yet, I do not find in either the Aarne-Thompson or the Thompson Indexes any tale remotely like my mother's. This is not to say that an analog will not appear, nor that I would be surprised if one did. My mother's tale might then be simply a case of an actual event prompting the weaving of a new fabric from old traditional story threads. But with or without analogs from wherever or whenever, the tale as my mother has told it is thoroughly Near Eastern. The early bethrothal, the coin-pledge ceremony, the intense family loyalty, the shooting of guns in celebration, even the poetic imagination of the young lover reminiscent of the colorations of the *Song of Songs*, are all from the value system, the social ethos, with respect to family and place, of the Lebanese Mountain specifically and the Near East generally. The story pattern of a misunderstanding precipitating a feud concerning family honor of course is an archetypal mythos in Near Eastern, really in World Literature. However, one should note finally, my mother's story is not of individual tragedy, as the pattern often runs, but of social comedy.

Next a story of my mother's (actually her friend's as told to me by my mother), centered on that deepest obligation within the Lebanese family: the respect for parents and grandparents, for age in general, the supreme continuity-link in any social system, since we must all get old. The scene is of my mother's friend, Shafee'a, visiting to console my mother, Mintaha, who is grieving after the death of my father:

> "Stop, Mintaha! You will make me cry and I did not come to make a woman's concert. You must not cry when you have good sons! But wait, I have a story for you about a old lady in the old country who did not have good sons."
>
> "Can this be a story to make one laugh?"
>
> "We will see. The old lady was a widow and her children were married and neglected her so that she had little to eat and could hardly get out of bed."
>
> "*Ya Botille*! [such an ending] She would have been better off bringing up swine."
>
> "They were true swine but inedible. Her neighbor however was a good soul, but poor, and with many children. This honorable neighbor made up her mind to have the old woman fed by those damnable children in spite of themselves. So she visited next door and asked to borrow the old lady's best olive crock, which the old lady

gave her with all the usual blessings. And the woman sat down in front of her place and painted the crock gold. Now the first lady that went by of course wanted to know what she was doing and was told in all secrecy that the crock was to be filled with the old lady's treasure and buried in the cellar. Meantime, every night for two weeks the woman took the crock of gold to the outhouse and relieved herself in it, and then she buried it and its treasure in the old lady's cellar."

"A swine's treasure indeed."

"And so the children were always in the mother's house and the daughter-in-laws cooked and cleaned and combed their mother's hair and dressed her in the highest style. And the boys, those *ackroots*, [panderers] addressed their mother in high flown language, and she lived liked a queen for six years, for which she thanked God and died."

"Well, *yellah*, [let's go], the priest and the lawyer scrambled over to the house after the funeral ahead of the villagers and discovered that the old lady had not expressed her wishes about the disposal of the crock of gold. Priest, lawyer, and children argued the whole day (assisted by the villagers) but finally it was decided that the priest would get his tenth and the children would get equal portions of the rest except that the lawyer for his past and future services also deserved a bit of it. The lawyer in his wisdom suggested that the crock of gold be placed on his head (he had a very flat head) and it be broken with a stick, the treasure remaining on his head to be his. This was done with all haste, and lawyer, priest and living children all got their rightful share of the treasure."

"This is a story, Shafee'a, that should be taught in all schools..."

This was the kind of story calculated to cheer up the disconsolate: an affirmation of the cultural ethic with respect to age and family behavior, of the taboo against the breaking of the family circle, all affirmed through the immense vitality of Shafee'a's joyful idiom, her ironies bristling with scornful understanding. The abhorrence of my parents' generation of what they called the old peoples' home, which they found in America, was absolute, a symbol for what would be the total disintegration of their village culture, a place, where, as they said, parents were gathered together like old dogs and piled up to die in one building.

The story is, too, a comic affirmation in such a family-oriented society, of what they felt was a healthy suspicion of those outside the circle, even of clergy, who could at times be less than holy, and especially of those whom I have translated as lawyers, but what is in Arabic "sheik," meaning the Ottomon-appointed village administrator of Turkish Law. The bad spiritual and secular administrators get what they deserve, as do the bad children: thus the moral longings of a traditional society.

I was perhaps introduced to the comparative study of folklore when as a teenager I arrived early for a movie date with an Italian-American girl in East Utica and was entertained with stories by her grandfather. He told me a story about a crock of gold, much like my mother's story, from his repertoire of Sicilian village stories from before W.W.I., and to the same end: the affirmation of family obligation. I remember being somewhat shocked, wondering if perhaps my mother or her pal Shafee'a had gotten the story from one of their Italian neighbors. I wanted it, of course, to be the other way around, that these Lebanese immigrants, masters of the moral life as I saw them, be the Sicilians' teachers, not their students. It was quite possible that the story flowed from one immigrant group to another in East Utica. This is how stories have spread -- diffusion is the term the folklorists use -- from the dawn of human history. And after all, my ancestors, the Phoenicians -- as my people love to point out -- had their part in the diffusion of Near Eastern culture to the early Greeks. And then, of course, there were the Crusades, where the Christian Europeans interacted with the Christian Lebanese...But I know enough now about the history of this tale to realize that my parent's generation and that of the old Sicilian probably received some version of the tale independently, from their own ancestral sources. Let me quote *verbatim* the citation in the Thompson *Motif-Index*:

P236.2. *Supposed chest of gold induces chilren to care for aged father*. They think that the chest of stones contains the inheritance. *Pauli (ed. Bolte) No. 435; Scala Celi 98b No. 528; Dunlop-Wilson II 185f.; von der Hagen II lviii   No. 49: Hdwb. d. Abergl. IV 1290.--Lithuanian: Balys Index No. 2452*; Spanish : Boggs FFC XC 116 No. 980A; Italian Novella: *Rotunda; Palestine: Schmidt-Kahle Volkserzählungen aus Palästina II No. 123; India: *Thompson-Balys; Indonesia: Jeynball Catalogus Maleische en Sundaneesche Hss. 173, ibid.   Supplement Catalogus Javaansche en Madoereesche Hss. 22.

The deception of one's children to induce proper behavior is apparently a "universal" motif found in the tales of many lands over many centuries. I won't pretend to have read the citations listed, but it is apparent that by introducing the helpful neighbor in the Lebanese version added pathos is generated by having the mother simply the victim of her children rather than have her clever in her own interests. Though the *Motif-Index* has many citations for "excrement," there are none for any plot line remotely like this one. And while folktale has endless examples of bad or foolish priests and civil village officials, none seem to have been humiliated in just the manner of this tale. The originality of some of the motifs or blending of motifs that seem apparent in this tale might still be illusory; perhaps close analogs may be (have been?) found. No matter, the tale as it stands, as delivered by Shafee'a and my mother, is radiant with the village values, the ethos, of their time and place. The text of the tale can then stand as a paradigm of a village unique in its time, place, and language, yet, one must add, much like other villages of other times, places, and languages.

Never would I have suspected as a youngster (nor of course would she have) that my mother's tale of a too-clever and avaricious priest in the old country would have been composed of motifs from ancient times and faraway countries, but then again, now that I do know (and I admit to prejudice), her tonality and her additions (if they are additions) seem to me to have greatly enriched the tale:

> There was a peasant in the old country who had a wife and eight children and one cow. From this cow they got milk and cheese and butter, enough to live from day to day. The peasant and his wife prayed incessantly that their lot be bettered. But the village priest had that typical frailty of man - covetousness - and could not bear that any cow be eating grass outside the fences of the church pasture. So on a Sunday at the pulpit, the priest turned directly to the peasant and spoke the words of the gospel that he who gives to God and His church of his house or his cow will have his gift returned to him three and four fold. The simple peasant saw the end to his misery and

determined to give his cow to the church, whereupon his wife shrieked and his children wept. But he gave the cow to the priest (who accepted it with humility and grace) and went home in a blessed mood to await his fortune.

The peasant's cow felt out of place among the clergy's cattle and too confined. Late at night it broke through the fence and for some reason the priest's cows followed. The peasant on his mattress on the floor of his place was awake and heard the pounding of hoofs. He looked out of the window on the moonlit night and saw his little yard full of cattle. He roused his wife and cried, "It has happened my dear wife, it has happened. The Lord has given us twelve cows for one."

This village Man of God was wild in the morning and rushed to the peasant's yard. "It has happened, Father, as you promised," said the peasant. Our father had to think. The shepherd found the perfect solution for this member of his flock. "My uncle," said the priest, "God will tell us who deserves these cows. Whoever rises first in the morning and says 'Good morning' first to the other shall keep them." The sly priest was sure the peasant did not know that the morning began at midnight, and he was right. But the peasant had a plan of his own.

The peasant slept that night in the tree by the priest's house and placed an empty kettle at the door. Close to midnight the priest quietly arose, slipped out the door and knocked over the kettle. The peasant awoke and cried out "Good Morning, Father, what the devil time is this to be out?"

The first half of the tale (till the cows come home) I have since found is a motif separately and brilliantly told by Jean Bodel of Arras, one of the first writers of fabliaux at the turn of the thirteenth century (see "Brunain, the Priest's Cow" in *Fabliaux*, ed. Hellmann & O'Gorman, 1965, pp. 27-9). Borel's version is close in content and tone to the version above save that in the Borel the peasant's wife is agreeable to giving the cow to the priest. This motif is Thompson's K366.1.1, where, however, the peasant is a "trickster." The second half of the tale, involved with the "good morning" bargain (Aarne 1735, Thompson K176), has the "trickster" catch the priest in a sexual encounter with his housekeeper, who then buys the peasant's silence with the return of his cow. In my mother's version the empty-kettle-at-the-door motif allows the peasant to remain pious, to be clever, but not a trickster. My mother's version of the tale does not revolve around a sexual indiscretion, but a battle of wits between two peasants, one a clergyman. The situation as presented in my mother's version is a good mirror of the state of affairs in the Christian Lebanon Mountain of, say, 1910, where the village clergy were largely of the peasantry and not very much more educated than their flock. It renders both the typical piety and respect of the Lebanese

Mountaineer, but also his sophistication concerning human frailty. In the words of the proverb my father loved to quote, "a wide cleft there is between the Divine and the human."

I have a related tale on tape of another poor village priest and his flock told not by my mother but by the late esteemed poet of the Lebanese community of East Utica, Adbullah Maroon, who was both master of a brand of improvisational poetry and a spellbinder of a storyteller. I have an hour's tape of his singing in verse (often on topics called for impromptu from the audience) and his storytelling at a wedding celebration in the 1950's, after he had been well lubricated with *Arak*, the Lebanese grape alcohol flavored with anise:

> Once in the old country was a priest in a little village in the Mountain whose flock was drifting away from him a bit, together of course with their fleece, and, for whatever reason it was happening, he knew that something drastic had to be done. He promised at the Sunday pulpit a miracle for his people on the following Thursday, and then set about to think of how the devil to make one.
>
> And as he walked and meditated, he found in his path sleeping by the road a young man well known for his gambling and idleness. All at once the answer came to him.
>
> "My son, would you do me a service for two whole dollars?"
>
> "Anything, Father, anything you say."

"What it seems I need is to put a beard on you and to have you hang nailed on a cross up on the church wall from time to time for a few days."

"But Father, nails in my hands and feet!"

"No, no, we will put nails between your fingers and put a little blood of a lamb on your hands and feet."

And so the youth was put up there on the wall after the morning mass on Thursday, and the people came after lunch as the priest had asked. He addressed them thus at the church door:

"O my people, I have the miracle I promised you, and more blessed is it than I ever dreamed. The Lord has honored our humble village with a manifestation of His dear Son on the cross. May this miracle strengthen your faith, and demonstrate to you once and for all that your pastor is a true priest."

And in he led his flock, which gasped at the sight, the young man on the wall opening his eyes only a little crack.

"In the name of the Father and the Son and the Holy Ghost! O my Lord, you know what is in my heart! A thousand thanks for coming to us, a poor people. What I ask you now, O Lord, is to listen in your mercy to the petitions of your flock. Is that all right with you, Lord?"

And the young man nodded his head.

"I saw him move, I saw it!" screamed a lady.

"I saw it too," said another.

The young man closed his eyes as if in pain, though in his heart was laughter.

"O Lord, please see to it that my daughter have a son the next time!"

The young man nodded.

"O my God, let my secret wish be granted!" said a young girl.

The young man nodded. And then to the front came Brigitta.

"*Ya Rabbi, ya Rabbi,* be so kind as to give me, give me now five hundred dollars in cash that I might straightaway pay off my mortgage!"

The young man opened his eyes wide with anger and shouted:

"God damn the bones of your fathers! You're crying for five hundred dollars and here I am hanging for three days for a lousy two bucks!"

"Brigitta" was Abdullah's constant foil, almost as witty and as good a poet as Abdullah, but not quite. I remember audiences of Abdullah's generation transfixed by his songs and stories of their old country villages, which seemed always spontaneous, new, and original. But as with all improvisation, the base of the art was traditional, with the genius in the flashes of originality, the twisting of the old traditional motifs into a new, often ironic, context.

Thompson's *Motif-Index* has but one citation of a tale like Abdullah's, but it is quite close: "L435.4. The beggar on the cross in place of Christ. Is made to leave the cross for his impatience concerning the sinners. Lithuanian: Balys Index No. 800A." My guess is that Abdullah, who was one of the few in the community who could read literary Arabic, got the story from a written Arabic collection, giving it, of course, his own tone and embellishment to fit his audiences' desire for their village culture.

The motif of the beggar's anger at the petitioners incidentally finds a masterful analog in Sancho Panza's anger at the aforementioned farmer from Miguelturra, who wanted to marry off his "handsome" son and asks Governor Sancho for 600 ducats to make up a dowry:

> "I swear, Don Country Bumpkin!" he cried, "if you don't get out of my sight at once, you unmannerly lout, and go hide yourself somewhere, I'll take this chair and lay your head wide open! Son of a whore, rascal, devil's painter! Is this any time to come asking me for six hundred ducats? Where would I get them, you stinking cur? ...Tell me, you wretch: I've not had the government a day and a half yet, and where do you expect me to lay hands on six hundred ducats?"

Salvatore Salomone-Marino in his *Customs and Habits of the Sicilian Peasants* (1897) has a lovely paraphrase of what he calls a typical Sunday sermon of an impoverished village clergyman. It could as well have come from Abdullah's foxy priest:

> Now you, you all do the opposite from the precepts and examples of the Divine Master, who seems to have left his parables more for the sake of the Turks and Protestants than for you: the reason is you are indifferent, ungrateful, ill-mannered, etc., etc, Tell, me, does it seem right to you, does it seem holy to let God's house go to ruin, and what do His ministers matter? The church, mind you, is bare; the walls are crumbling, the roof threatens to cave in! If you do not provide for this as well as for me, the ruins can fall down on our necks, and then who do you expect will provide? Me, perhaps? I, as you know, am poor, poor to the point that I have to wear patched clothes and a hat worn thin and full of holes.
> (English edition, 1981, p. 117)

And yet, says Salomone-Marino generally of these clergy (and their parishioners):

> they are compassionate, and because they are men of the world, they understand human frailty; and they enjoy the respect and love of the parishioners, who willingly and ceaselessly, although sparingly, support them, while smiling mischievously at the ever-same Sunday sermons.
> (p. 119)

This, I would say, is also the right tone to define the relationship of village clergy to parishioners in Mount

Lebanon of the same time period, as I sense it from many of the stories of my mother and father's generation. The priest was after all one of them, even God was one of them ("God is fresh" my mother used to say, "that he never gave me a daughter"), a distant Uncle Who visited the village at will. And while perhaps God had no frailties, according to my mother the saints who founded the three major Christian sects in Lebanon surely did:

> Specially revered by the Maronites is St. M'rite, by the Melkites St. M'ran and by the Roum St. Inoula. And it happened that even these fell to squabbling - in my hometown, I think it was - way back in the old days, about who was closer to the good God. And, as Arabs, they were all quick tempered and they fell to fighting. M'ran delivered M'rite a fist in the right eye, unfortunately blinding him. Inoula took a stick and gave M'ran a crack in the shin bone, which was sadly never to heal right. And finally M'rite levied a kick to the groin of Inoula, which alas precipitated a rupture which would torment Inoula from that day on. And so it was that M'rite went about blinking, blind in one eye, M'ran limped, and Inoula hobbled. So it is that we children of the Saints, and weaker than they, fight now over nothing of importance.

One wonders if this folk allegory is not so specific to the confessional situation in Lebanon that it is uniquely of that place, or whether it is but a modification of motifs concerning squabbling drawn from universal folk literature motifs. One soon ceases to care, so right are the comic, absurd images of the squabbling, so right is the moral, the village wisdom, for that Lebanese situation, that we are satisfied with the brief aesthetic moment, however or wherever derived.

I recall a similar moment when, as a college boy home for the summer and in the company of my two older brothers around the kitchen table, I pressed our mother (as we always did) for a story. I was so pleased then both with the story and the conversation it elicited, that I put it all down that evening in my notebook:

- I will tell you a story, in Arabic, about laziness, to keep my sons from getting lazy.

A man and his wife were laying in bed in the old country in the old days and the light was on and the door was open. And they were both lazy. "My dear wife, my sweet fig, be so kind as to shut the light and fasten the door" said the husband. "My heart's desire, my breath; please do it yourself as I am very tired," replied his wife. And so they talked till they both fell asleep and the door was wide open and the light was on. This was the time of the Turks, so here comes a Turk on his horse late at night and both man and horse tired and hungry. He kicked the door and roared to the man and his wife, "I am hungry, I want food and drink for myself and my horse!" He waved his sword and the man and wife jumped quickly up. The man said, "We are poor, we have only lentils and hay." The Turk replied, "I will have chicken and my horse will have clover; I know you have both. And a salad and some rice, coffee and baklawa, will do nicely. Arak also. Quick." And the man and his wife ran back and forth in the house and out of the house, to the table and to the horse in the field, and prepared a banquet. The Turk sat down but he would not eat alone and demanded that they eat and drink with him. And when he was thoroughly drunk he waved his sword and ordered that the wife dance and the husband sing. And they had to. So it was that in the late night the wife rose and began to dance and the husband wailed and sang these words:

> My wife, had you closed the door
> You would not have been brought so low
> You would not have had to stamp the floor
> Nor would I have been forced to crow.

The brothers found that the story had the stuff of real laughter but debated whether the key was in the sequence of events or in their embellishment by the Teller, or primarily in the final image, whether, that is, the rightness of such a tale was a contextual or an archetypal affair. (The debate was languid rather than fervent.) The youngest asserted that in any case the man singing and his wife dancing would remain in his mind as an image as strong as Wordsworth's solitary reaper singing alone. The question, however, of whether it ought to was as quickly broached as dismissed as outside the realm of criticism. The mother told her sons flatly that the story was good because lazy people were made to look ridiculous, but her sons agreed that this was facile and encouraged their mother to stay within the artist's realm.

As well she should, for the realm of analysis cannot make such a story come into being. Criticism can however appreciate it, can relate its motifs to others like it, its figurations to other works of the past and present, derive its specific historical context in 19th century Lebanon, and its ethical positions in terms of its social context in Lebanon (or in East Utica). It may well have originated in a true incident in Mt. Lebanon, and then been crafted using traditional materials from previous centuries. It seems, finally, to this observer that knowing the traditional materials that go into a given piece of folk literature such as this is helpful mostly in explaining discontinuities that one might sense in the tale. When however everything seems right in a tale, in style, content and tone, when it beautifully illuminates a given social context, a place and a people, the study of the traditional sources and analogs certainly must take second place to the pleasures of the unique aesthetic moment.

My mother's tape recording and Abdullah's likewise actually have more folk poetry on them than folktale, and whether it be my mother's traditional lyrics or Abdullah's semi-improvisations, the sense of family and place is equally at the heart of most of the poems. Abdullah and my mother shared the intense love for the same village (they were neighbors in the old country), the Wadi El Arayesh ("Valley of the Grapevines"), which was a tiny hill village adjoining the larger town, Zahle. Zahle was my father's village, a resort town famed for its open air restaurants nestled in a ravine along a cool mountain stream. In my *Wind of the Land* I describe as follows a typical evening gathering of my youth:

> *Sahrah* in the dilapidated East Utica hall, 1955, the arak flowing, the hour late. The song and the dance having tired the people, they called for poetry. It was Abdullah Maroon they wanted, for improvisations to cheer or weep over, to soften and make more delicate the heart. And laugh and cheer and weep they did, for an hour that seemed a moment. One knew Abdullah's feeling when he finally returned in his poems to his own village:

oof, oof, oof. (as he meditates)
Wadi El Arayesh,
Wadi El Arayesh,
Grapes of perfection cover your valley.
Pluck, O my villagers, and taste them,
One by one.

And the people thrill to the pain. It was the bittersweet pain of emigrees that found its quintessential expression (at least for my parents and their fellow villagers) in a popular Lebanese folk song sung usually by a soloist alternating with the audience as chorus (my translations here and below):

She:
O you who have your lovers!
My lover is gone.
O God! Turn the wind round
And bring my lover back.

Chorus:
Al-Rosanna, Al-Rosanna,
All pleasures are in her.
What did Rosanna do
That you have punished her?

She:
I would climb to the top of the mountain
And look down on the Wadi
And say, "How welcome
The breeze from our village."

"Beirut, I would not live in you,
Your heat would stifle me.
Zahle, my desire,
In you my lover dwells."

O you who have your lovers!
   & etc.

Chorus:
Al-Rosanna, Al-Rosanna
   & etc.

She:
He asked me for a kiss
I said "Go way, you Madman,
We Arab girls
Walk in Independence!"

In our garden is an apricot,
In his family's garden is a plum
The shadow of the plum
Touches the apricot.

O you who have your lovers!
   & etc.

Chorus:
Al-Rosanna, Al-Rosanna
   & etc.

She:
O you merchants on the road to Aleppo
My lover is gone before you
You bearing the delicate grape
And the sweet, firm apples beneath them.

O you who have your lovers!
   & etc.

Chorus:
Al-Rosanna, Al-Rosanna
   & etc.

The lover's passion, expressed in the touch of the shadows of the fruit trees, and of the grapes and the apples, is tempered by the pride of the woman who spurns the improper advance. The singer's passion for her lover is equalled by her love for her village, the Wadi or Zahle, and its cool breezes, as contrasted to the heat of the alien city of the plain, Beirut (of 1910). One need not come from the Wadi or Zahle to feel the spirit of the *Jabeleeyee*, or mountain folk of Mt. Lebanon, for such feelings of passion and pride, localism and familialism, are indigenous to mountain folk cultures throughout time. Witness again (p. 58) the *Song of Songs*:

Come with me from Lebanon, my spouse, with me from Lebanon: look from the top of Amana, from the top of Shenir and Hermon,...

A fountain of gardens, a well of living waters,
and streams from Lebanon.

I visited Lebanon only the once and briefly in 1960, before the inferno with which it has been afflicted, and walked the paths of my parent's village. At a party in my honor in a grove in the evening, one of my cousins sang a traditional song, as the villagers, many of them my cousins, danced arm in arm in a long line:

Your hand, my darling.
We to lead and they to follow
Take the hand and toe the earth
With anyone that rises.

God will witness as we dance
And He will judge if it be good
We will thank God as we dance
That we have you back again.

Dear, you left us, and now are here
When you left, the stars rained blood
Now you ask us who we are!
Your loved ones, dear, who live again.

I will sing until I tire
Then someone will sing for me
Zahle's heart was burning for you
The maiden eager for her sons.

So, my eyes, again we see you

And once more have come to life
Ahlan wa Sahlan to you
You have come into our hearts.

I had never been to this village or society, much less left it, but my parents had, of course, and stories of their childhood in the village were still remembered by my relatives in the village. "The stars rained blood" is not my metaphor, but theirs; likewise the term, "my eyes." The personification of their village, Zahle, as passionate mother is traditional, as are the figurations of death and resurrection. The evening was in fact ended by another relative singing another traditional folk song to me which was also of death and resurrection. It uses in addition the traditional image of the blessed wind, or *hawa*, as both a physical and spiritual wind:

> We died, and are born again
> From this wind of our land
>
> I sing for you at evening
> Here in the shade and shadow
>
> Your sun shines on me now
> And out of a grave my bones are risen
>
> When you leave the day darkens
> My heart sinks and dies
>
> You had gone, and are come again
> Welcome to you, and more than welcome

O, my loved one...

We died, and are born again
From this wind of our land

Presumably I, or any visiting relative, was the wind and sun returning to the village. I could not help but have feelings of confusion when I heard these words, as I thought both of their aptness and inaptness. In what way was I bringing vitality to them? Were they not, in their social solidarity, bringing vitality to me? It is a question I have often asked myself since, even in these dark days for Lebanon. And I think often of this song's poignant effect on the Lebanese immigrants of East Utica many years ago, as the song itself became a breath of their old country village and its vitality as they sang it. Thus the title of my memoir, *Wind of the Land*.

Folk poetry, perhaps by definition, is intensely communal, appreciated and practiced by a good number within the given society. Abdullah tells the following anecdote on tape:

> Once in the old country on the hill path up from Zahle to the vineyards, I found Brigitta, the old lady, by the gate to her garden.
>
> "Ya Maroon my son, I have some verses for you that I have just put together as I saw you coming."
>
> "I stand, my dear Aunt, waiting."

> oof, oof, oof.
> O my eyes, my noble Maroon, *salaam*!
> You were blessed with song from your mother's womb.
> You've a mind like the mind of the wise Hillel,
> And a head as big and as hard as a mule's.

"Thank you, mother, and now I must answer you in verse."
"I stand waiting, my son."

> oof, oof, off.
> O Lady Brigitta, with these words,
> So elegantly turned and mixed, I compare
> The dirty white of the smoke of a train:
> Noxious at first, and then nothing at all.

And I have heard tell of a summer's regional picnic (*mahrajan*, the Lebanese call it) where Abdullah compared the verses of another folk poet to dirty linen in need of the services of the local Chinaman. Salomone-Marino has some wonderful examples of such folk song competition amongst the Sicilian peasantry at communal agricultural festivals throughout the year, including contests in improvisation, introduced typically in this way:

> A: She who dares, let her try to contrast.
>   Let fire her voice and try to compete in song.

> a: I dare, and I really come to contrast;
> Fire off then, as I shall compete with you in song.
> A: Have a care, do not fly so high, lower your wings,
> Better watch that you do not tumble headlong!
> a: High and wide I do handsomely spread my wings,
> Securely I fly, I go right to the sun!

Woe to the storyteller who is not up to the competition:

> The rustic Andrea Albano, one night in November 1853, in the ex-fief Pignicello, mocked his companion Benedetto as Little Snail, who clumsily recounted childish little stories, with the following satirical poem:
>
> Zu 'Biaidi', I bend to salute you.
> You are my master; I am at your feet;
> Blessed that remarkable mother
> Who taught you these very learned tales!
> A fine storyteller, and likewise sower,
> Who speaks to men eloquently;
> Then you can pleasure old men and children
> With the little tale-*once upon a time a barber*....

But, finally, whether good or bad, in Sicily (or in Lebanon) at the turn of the century, there was nothing more loved by the peasantry than poetry:

> And if by chance there is a poet in the group, he is asked and tricked into composing verses, which are then applauded noisily by all, even when not so good,

so as to encourage him not give up readily... no entertainment is so pleasing to our peasants as that which gives exercise in composing and reciting poetry, especially the improvised kind.

Abdullah peddled bananas from a beat-up truck for a living and had no money; when he was asked to travel all over the United States to sing at weddings, funerals, and births, he asked only for train fare and *arak*. His poetry was like prophecy to the Lebanese; few were born with the inventiveness, the inspiration, the wit. But as for the simple poetization of life and language, I found it everywhere in the Arabic speech of the old immigrants of my parent's generation. The following is from a listing I made once in my notebook:

> "Beauty is spring water gushing from the rock," says Yusef Elasmar, "and the good man's thirst quenched." "The apricot in flower and the wind through it," says my father. "A young girl's pomegranate cheeks and almond eyes, that's what beauty is," says Abdullah. "The *Quoddous* of the mass," said Father Bschara long ago, "I can never keep from crying."

Beauty in the remembered landscapes of their locale and in the harmonies of the sect in which they found their identity. Also in their home and village gardens, which they invested with their own identities. Here again from my notebook, my mother and father in our backyard in East Utica:

"Ya Mike, our uncle the pear has been giving rich beautiful fruit without a spot for the thirty-three years we have been married. And all we do for him is bless him and fill the bushels. And the plum next to him is weak and we take the worms from his roots every year and he does not recover."

"Ya Mintaha, some bear and some do not bear; some live long and well, and some are weak and die quick. Nobody knows what is in the mind of the good God."

"Ya Mike, do you remember the great mulberry tree by your uncle's house in the Wadi? How we would all sit in it and eat and eat."

"I remember my Uncle Paul shouting to you in his loud voice 'Ya, Mintaha of the House of Kassouf, if you continue to eat of our Mulberry, you will have the blood of the Nassars in you and then you will have to marry Mike when you get older and make the graft complete!' And I said 'No, Uncle Paul, the Kassoufs have an Apricot, and you can't graft an apricot to a mulberry.'"

"And what do you now say, ya Mike?"

This is an example of natural myth-making, metaphor becoming symbol through the intensity of the feeling and its congruence both with the ethos of a people and its spiritualized landscapes. That ethos, so involved with family and place and God of place, can be symbolized in the great mulberry tree, as above, or as I have stressed earlier (p. 13), in the humble lettuce leaf in the traditional folk song as sung by my mother, with which I began these essays:

> The roses are full, full
> The roses are always on my mind.
> I love the roses only,
> And, O my soul, the lettuce leaf.

If this little lyric has for the reader some of the feeling of haiku, I am glad, since it has always seemed to me to demonstrate the delicacy of sensibility of the best of peasant village culture, East or West, from earliest times to the present. The lettuce leaf surprises the reader, perhaps, till he realizes he is being forced to recognize the primacy of the commonplace and therewith a common humanity, the ideal of universality and centrality at the core of human experience.

It is at the level of the village, the neighborhood, or at most the region, and its families, that most of us can cope with alienation, there where a lovely social context can be formed and maintained. The fears of the Lebanese immigrant to the United States, as the fears of any emigrees, was that the New Country with all its centrifugal forces, would crush the family and obliterate its past. At the end of my *Wind of the Land*, I have a long poem, largely of my own composing, though based on a recollection of a formal declamation of one of the community's folk poets (not Abdullah but Yusef Elasmar), who formulated the issues always discussed back then by my parent's generation, as well as the answers always given. These are the opening stanzas:

> Where is the America of our dreams, O brothers of my generation?
> And the America of your dreams, O children of my brothers?
> Where it always was, O brothers, in the hearts of our fathers,
> In the acts of the good man who looks to his children,
> In the joy of the child in the lap of his grandmother.
> Filiality is the base of all good dreams.
>
> America has indeed been lavish in the casting of flowers,
> Of flowers that do not grow in the old country villages,
> Generous, open, accessible in the highest of glories.
> But what of the flowers, the country flowers of the village,
> Simplicity, serenity, and joy, the sense of belonging?

Michael Novak, the ethical and ethnic philosopher (see above, page 43), has lamented that the family has been out of favor with social planners in the West. What has been the radiant core of Western (and Eastern) Civilization is sometimes seen as an archaic, irrational and disruptive form of social organization. I cannot disagree that there is a darker side to the idyllic vision of family and village or neighborhood life in which these folktales and folksongs find their reference, especially in considering the last nightmarish decades in Lebanon, full of brutality and fear. But then, too, I remember the joy and the tears in my father's eyes as he listened to a folk tale told or a folk song sung about his village, and I question if we have really any adequate substitute for the village dream, for the clan together beneath the grapevine, within hearing of the church bell.

Chapter Four

Social Contexts as Poetic Texts

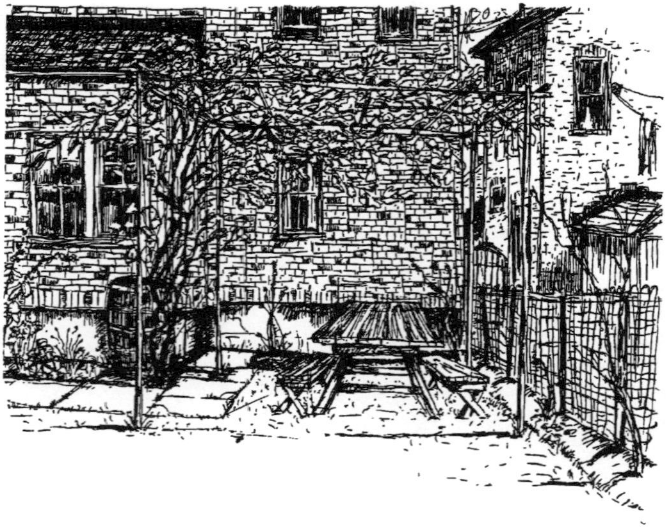

All good things have their tragic obverse. In considering the literature of the *Old Testament* from the viewpoints of Familialism and Localism in Chapter Two, I alluded to the tragic events presently occurring, as they have always occurred, in the geographic area of the *Bible*. The various populaces of the region down through history (excluding the privileged) have rarely had anything other than the satisfactions of family and place and faith to sustain them. Magnificent social cultures have sprung therefrom, as well as bitter internecine rivalries.

The Lebanese Mountain villagers (my people) were starved by the Turks in the First World War and lost one-third of its million people. The Germans killed six million Jews in Europe, and a portion of the survivors returned to the ancestral home of nineteen hundred years previous, supplanting more than six-hundred thousand of the indigenous Palestinians. One portion then of the Palestinian Diaspora have found themselves in misery and brought misery upon the indigenous peoples of neighboring Lebanon. These facts thud on the mind as an endless march of human suffering. The exclusivist spirit of German Nationalism exerted all the pressure within its power upon the unwanted Jews; the Jews press upon the Palestinians, the Palestinians upon the Lebanese, who, of course, press back. People all of high cultures, the Germanic, the Hebraic, and the Christian and Islamic

Arabic, peoples capable of high admiration for each other's culture, and capable at the same time of the most corrosive hatreds. The fault is in the cultures, ultimately in ourselves, and not likely to be easily eradicable. It needs to be admitted: there is in mankind considered generally, in all the peoples of mankind, the capacity to kill whole groups of people not of one's group. The Germanic peoples can be moved to kill all the Jews (or Slavs, or whomever), the Turks all the Lebanese (or Armenians, or whomever). It can hardly be doubted that any people can be moved to kill all the people of any other group. Given another Masada, the Jews would use a nuclear bomb on the Palestinians, or whomever, just as surely as the Palestinians, or whoever, sufficiently humiliated and sufficiently armed, would use a nuclear bomb, or whatever, on the Jews. Whoever wants the beautiful hills of Lebanon will destroy the indigenous peoples of Lebanon, given sufficient motivational energy, excuse, and opportunity. The Lebanese, being weak and fragmented, will probably go on being victims, but are quite capable of ferociously killing one another, given the guns and the leeway. Does anyone really doubt this darkness in the human spirit, at least when one is speaking generally about masses or "herds" of peoples? It is too common in history, ancient and modern, to doubt.

No doubt too that it is but a small proportion of a people that have true evil in their individual hearts, however produced. One might even wonder if there is such a thing as unconditional evil, whether, that is, Hitler might have been, in different circumstances, merely a mean-spirited shopkeeper, Stalin a bluff grandfather,

Mengele a respected doctor in Germany, or Kurtz (of Conrad's *Heart of Darkness*) a respectable businessman, pious and eloquent, in Belgium.

One can be full of fanaticism, as Hitler, and do evil, or be so empty, so alienated, so nihilistic, as to do evil, as Dostoyevski's Raskolnikov and Camus's outsider, who murder from emptiness. The mob or the mass or the herd, however, cannot think or act as a group without some adherence to some exclusivist doctrine which defines the group. The herd instinct and the howling of the mob are frightening, and become more so when one realizes that, most likely, there is a trigger for the instinct somewhere in one's own personality that will make him run with one herd or another at one time or in one set of circumstances or another. One hopes that one will be lucky enough to avoid such a triggering towards a truly evil act in one's lifetime, that he might be kept from the heart of darkness, the void, the emptiness within, or from some context of violent fanaticism to one cause or another without. Perhaps, too, there are those of true goodness, who do not need luck to remain good; perhaps a Saint Francis, or a Mother Teresa, or a Confucius, would be what they have been in any circumstances.

But for most of us, it is good luck, the good fortune to be in good circumstances, which allows us at least to avoid evil, or, if we are aiming higher, allows us to follow a light within, to feed a hunger within, towards goodness, that may be in some of us. Henry Fielding, in the passage from *Tom Jones* which I quoted earlier (p. 86), speaks of this hunger:

> There is in some (I believe in many) human breasts a kind and benevolent disposition, which is gratified by contributing to the happiness of others. That in this gratification alone, as in friendship, in parental and filial affection, as indeed in general philanthropy, there is a great and exquisite delight.

I have found this disposition in many of the people I have met from all nations and all walks of life. One sees it in the eyes of the persons, in their gestures, and of course in their actions. I have seen it in the eyes of a Japanese friend at Kenyon College, and in the eyes of the mother of a Nepalese friend at Oxford University. One comes to believe in a community of sympathy beyond cultural boundaries, a community of people of kind disposition from every village on the earth. These are the people one lives for; these are the true friends, and one is blessed in knowing them.

But blessings must be saved too for the given culture or society which keeps one either from the void of alienation or anomie or from the fanatic statism that worships one's nation exclusively. And it is of these latter blessings that I want, after some preliminaries, to speak in this concluding chapter.

I have written elsewhere (as well as in the chapters above) of the proper critical approach to the study of societies, which, I have argued, is not essentially different from the proper critical approach to literary texts (see "Contextualism in Art and Life: Social Criticism," in my *Essays Critical and Metacritical*, 1983). Simone Weil is acutely aware in her *The Need for Roots* (1952) of the blessings of a rooted society and of the obverse, the evils of tyrannical societies:

> The degree of respect owing to human collectivities is a very high one...each one is unique, and, if destroyed, cannot be replaced...The food that collectivity supplies, for the souls of those who form a part of it has no equivalent in the entire universe...But...it very often happens that the roles are reversed. There are collectivities which, instead of serving as food, do just the opposite: they devour souls.

Each "collectivity" is unique, as each literary text is unique. Each needs to be analyzed not on the critic's terms (such metacritical evaluation will certainly come later), but on its own terms. Michael Walzer, in his *Interpretation and Social Criticism* (1987), compares in a precise and fruitful way the jobs of the good literary and the good social critic:

> we are all interpreters of the morality we share...The best reading is not different in kind, but in quality, from the other readings: it illuminates the poem in a more powerful and persuasive way...The case is the same with moral interpretation: it will sometimes confirm and sometimes challenge received opinion. And if we disagree with either the confirmation or the challenge, there is nothing to do but go back to the "text"- the values, principles, codes, and conventions that constitute the moral world...

The implication here incidentally is that the given literary text is as ontologically "real" as the given society, a point which will not be conceded by the "deconstructive" critic of Chapter One (pp. 27 ff), who would also deny the reality of "better" or "worse" readings of the unique "text." I agree with Walzer's position, as well as with his further assertion that "good social criticism is as rare as good poetry or good philosophy".

What constitutes the better society? The most important point that needs to be made here is that just as with the great body of successful poems, there are any number of (or possibilities for) successful societies, all different from one another. The idea of a millennialist society at the end of, say, a Marxist or any other Monist road is as stifling as the idea of an Ultimate Poem, which will subsume all other poems. At the very least, the better society will have tolerance for other societies built on other values. At the same time, it will have a core structure of values which give meaning, coherence, and grace to daily living within that society. Durkheim's term for this structure is the "collective consciousness," which should not frighten one as the term "herd instinct" does. The social critic probes for the unique configuration of values in a unique society with more or less sensitivity.

How can we then speak of "human nature," given such a pluralistic mosaic of unique cultures? My previous chapters have addressed this question, and the answer is best found in the ideas of Charles Cooley, from whom the incisive quote on page 45 above, to which I refer the reader and to which needs to be added the following:

> What else can human nature be than a trait of primary groups?...it belongs...to man in association...We must see and feel the communal life of family and local groups as immediate facts, not as combinations of something else. And perhaps we shall do this best by recalling our own experience and extending it through sympathetic observation.

Men are most alike, have most to share, at the communal level of family, village, neighborhood, and region, and the similarity of sentiments generated by family and locale creates a communality, a centrality of outlook that can be called human nature. The idea is embraced by Jonathan Swift in his talk of "common forms" and Samuel Johnson in his of the "general truths of a common humanity" (see above, pp. 82 ff). W. H. Auden in his "In Praise of Limestone" expresses his deepest sympathies for the fluid limestone landscapes of his native Yorkshire and then extends his sympathies to any loved local landscape of common humanity and common forms, much as Thomas Mann does in *Tonio Kroger* for the "bliss of the commonplace," the "bourgeois love of the human, the living and usual" (above, p. 99 & 120). Such a sense of commonality and centrality is opposed to the singularity of nihilism, which fosters alienation and anomie, and of group fanaticism, which fosters exclusivism, the extremes at either end of the social spectrum.

Recalling one's own experience and extending it through sympathetic observation is clearly what is on W. H. Auden's mind and Thomas Mann's mind, and, I have tried to argue in my Chapter Two above, much on the minds of some major figures in world literature, for whom the values of familialism and localism are central. Certainly my own experience in growing up in a close Lebanese-American family in an Italian-American enclave in Upstate New York, has been, as I have argued throughout, absolutely crucial to my own intellectual and emotional life.

The blessings that I have experienced in my own social ambience are, to be sure (as are all such experiences), a blend of reality and imagination. It is compounded of the realities of good family, good friends, a neighborhood of some social continuity and grace (mixing two strong Mediterranean cultural traditions, the Lebanese Mountain and the Southern Italian), and a personal imagination hungry for symbols of order, harmony and permanence. Such symbols, as Wallace Stevens, among many others in our century, has taught us, may well be fictive, but none the less necessary to many, if not most, of mankind. We *will* sanctify local presences. Ezra Pound in his *Cantos* champions the myth-making capability in the mind, where in the past, "before ever dew was fallen," men had visions of gods:

Gods float in the azure air,
Bright gods and Tuscan, back before dew was shed.
(Canto 3)

I have always felt fortunate because on any given walk around my block or neighborhood I could, at any hour, spring or fall, meet friends with stories or invitations to coffee and treats, feel familiar with the cracks in a given sidewalk here or the bent weed there, sense the presence of people long gone walking and talking to me on street corners everywhere, God and vine and bird all intertwined in the shadows of my garden or the neighbor's garden, and sweet breezes everywhere floating from house to house, garden to garden.

No doubt but that the neighborhood can look completely desanctified to an outsider, or even to myself in a disaffected mood. Shall we define the imagination from when it seems half full or half empty? I have, to be sure, bad dreams, sleeping or waking, at times, counteracting my good dreams. I have dreamed at different times of house and garden decaying, the grape trellis buckling, the fruit trees withering, the rains crumbling the foundations of the house, the roof leaking, the porch wood rotting. And, of course, of family and friends come from the dead to complain of conditions of neglect there or here. But, then, one can repair the house in the sunshine of the day, and in spite of the death of family, friends, or of neighborhood or even cultural context, one can love the memories of family and place. And, if one is especially lucky, as I am lucky, one can see the kindness in one's father's eyes in the eyes of one's son, the gaiety in one's mother's eyes in the eyes of a younger daughter, and the wisdom in the eyes of an older brother in the eyes of an older daughter. All of these symbols that sustain one, these powerful presences that define one, that tell a person who he is, are both personal and unique, but also, if the person has some centrality to his experiences, teach him to know what human nature and the human heart is. One's block becomes the world, and one's neighborhood radiant with the core values of humanity. These are not intellectual responses to experience but emotional ones, and therefore are much more powerful, and meaningful to oneself than someone else's ideology. One builds an intellectual framework around such experience as one goes along.

One needs to have had the cultural context, and to have the imagination and memory, and then one needs to be lucky enough to not have the inevitable blows of reality be more than one can cope with. The village dream, a blessed order of a time and place, can be killed by events that cannot be assimilated into the dream. William Saroyan's Armenian Fresno of *My Name is Aram* might never be able to encompass the Armenian genocide of 1915 or the Armenian earthquake of 1988 for those who have survived these nightmares, but the book has enormous power as art for a sympathetic reader like myself who, like Saroyan, is mainly an observer to catastrophe.

My visit to Lebanon in 1960, described partially above, pp. 155 ff, seemed a dream of an earthly paradise, of a social culture so rich and rooted as to be inviolable, and against which the events of the '70's and '80's seem like the macabre fantasies of a madman. Bill Blakemore, the foreign correspondent for ABC News, spent some years teaching in Lebanon in the late '60's and his comments in *Aramco World* (July 1989) say beautifully very much what I have been trying to say about good societies and their tragic obverse:

> The 1960's were the days when Lebanon was the opposite of what it is now: it was in the days when Lebanon was self-consciously trying to be a witness to the world of how complexity can live in peace. There was an ideal alive which people were trying to live, the witness of Lebanon, which Fakreddine, the Druze leader, talked about four centuries ago. The late Charles Malek, the Lebanese Christian philosopher who was President of the United Nations General Assembly in 1959, talked about it. Sunni and Shite Muslim leaders I got to know later, as the civil war was first beginning, would talk about it. Peace and conflict are two sides of the same coin. So in a time when everybody wants to live in peace, and outside forces are not being too cynical, Lebanon is the most wonderful place. And it's the worst when the opposite holds.

And he goes on to say what I have been saying about the necessity (and inevitability) of repair, at the very least in the mind and imagination and memory. Blakemore on the country of my patrimony:

> People who follow news of the tragic developments in Lebanon from abroad might naturally assume that the kind of life I was so fortunate to experience there as a young teacher is gone forever. But Lebanon is an ancient land, a land of continuous change and flux, and it *is* coming back; I know that from history. We can read every week in the papers that the moment the

guns stop, it comes back. It's like a lovely, tenacious flower. Lebanon is always coming back; coming back is part of the spirit of the place.

I believe it, beyond all pessimism of other more topical commentators. The ancient village culture of the Lebanese Mountain, outlined in Chapter Three above, is of the order and beauty of a successful poem, and while most social contexts cannot match the longevity, the "permanence" of the greatest of poems, the most enduring of social contexts is certainly that of the peasant village. The similar traits, needs, continuities of the village culture--this book has argued-- has given rise to "human nature," and brought us to approaching, as a limit at least, the ideal of universality or centrality in human values.

That the existence of absolute human values cannot be defended philosophically is no more important to human need than that the existence of an absolute God or centering Force cannot be defended philosophically. The deconstructionists would claim that the impossibility of an absolute metaphysical grounding or centering renders language generally and analysis specifically, whether of the literary text or the social context, indeterminate. My position is, has always been, that one's hunger for a center, a focus, a meaning, an ordering, a continuity, will always draw him towards a center ("him" as mankind generally, including a good number of supreme artists), which center can be in art or religion or society, wherever. One shares (or at the very least can understand and analyze) a social, or a literary, context, a context which cannot pretend to absolute authority, which is partially a dream. Certainly the village, the poem, or the dream can be for the worse, or one can be living in a time of the tragic obverse of the dream, when a vile herd instinct is triggered, and the beneficent collective consciousness of a people is submerged. I have, however, been very lucky in the dreams in which I have found my own self-definition, and in the social context of family and place in which I have been privileged to live.